PRAISE

ESCAPE!
THE STORY OF THE GREAT HOUDINI
BY SID FLEISCHMAN

"[Fleischman's] rendering of the great Houdini is full-bodied and fresh, exuberant yet probing, meticulous and, yes, magical."—*San Francisco Chronicle*

"This absorbing biography of Houdini is . . . a fine example of creative nonfiction."
—*Seattle Times*

"Sid Fleischman . . . is a great entertainer in prose and his engaging account of Houdini's challenges, setbacks and triumphs rolls along in dramatic episodes, all punctuated with Sid's great wit and insight. . . . A welcome addition to the literature of both magic and popular culture."—*Magicol* Magazine

"[Sid Fleischman] is a born entertainer. . . . When he gets rolling he resembles nothing so much as an engaging carnival barker, with colorful similes and metaphors popping like flash pots, three to a page."
—*MUM: Society of American Magicians Magazine*

"Fleischman brings an insider's sensibility to Houdini's story . . . and brings readers along for an entertaining ride."—*Publishers Weekly* (starred review)

"Fleischman does the story of Houdini justice with an accessible, witty, and fascinating ride that is sure to draw in the skeptical and the admiring alike."
—*The Bulletin of the Center for Children's Books* (starred review)

(continued)

"The writing is fine, fluid, and engaging."—*VOYA*

"What do you get when you put two prestidigitators, one a spellbinding escape artist, the other a magician with words, into a black hat and wave the wand? Abracadabra—a feat that's pure magic."—*Kirkus Reviews* (starred review)

"Fleischman's tone is lively and he develops a relationship with readers by revealing just enough truth behind Houdini's 'razzle-dazzle' to keep the legend alive. . . . Engaging and fascinating."—*School Library Journal* (starred review)

"Readers will be fascinated."—ALA *Booklist* (starred review)

"The pacing is as sure and energetic as that of a practiced performer."
—*The Horn Book*

A *Boston Globe–Horn Book* Honor Book
An ALA Notable Book
An ALA Best Book for Young Adults
A *School Library Journal* Best Book
A *Publishers Weekly* Best Book
One of the New York Public Library's 100 Titles for Reading and Sharing
One of ALA *Booklist*'s Top 10 Youth Biographies
One of ALA *Booklist*'s Top 10 Arts Books for Youth

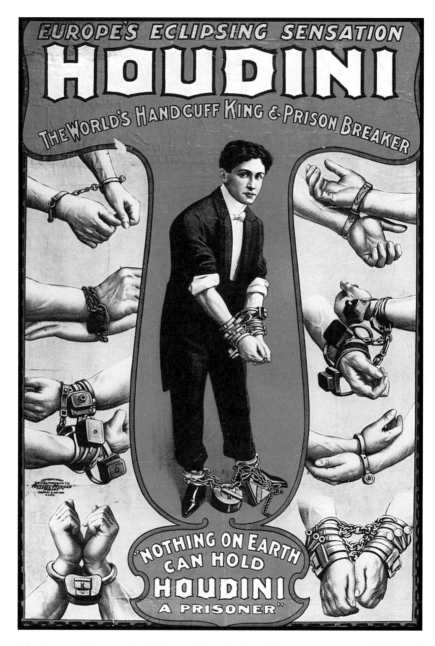

Having created a sensation in Europe, Houdini hoped this 1906 poster would kick off the same excitement in the United States. It didn't hurt. He was able to command a weekly salary of $1,200. To figure out what that would mean in today's dollars, calculate a century of inflation.

APE!
GREAT HOUDINI

SID FLEISCHMAN

GREENWILLOW BOOKS
An Imprint of HarperCollinsPublishers

Collins is an imprint of HarperCollins Publishers.

Escape! The Story of The Great Houdini
Copyright © 2006 by Sid Fleischman
Page 206 constitutes an extension of the copyright page.

Library of Congress Cataloging-in-Publication Data
Fleischman, Sid, (date).
Escape! : the story of the great Houdini / by Sid Fleischman.
p. cm.
"Greenwillow Books."
Includes bibliographical references.
ISBN 978-0-06-085094-4 (trade bdg.)
ISBN 978-0-06-085095-1 (lib. bdg.)
ISBN 978-0-06-085096-8 (pbk.)
1. Houdini, Harry, 1874-1926—Juvenile literature.
2. Magicians—United States—Biography—Juvenile literature.
3. Escape artists—United States—Biography—Juvenile literature.
I. Title.
GV1545.H8F55 2006 793.8′092—dc22 [B] 2005052631

Typography by Chad W. Beckerman

First Collins edition, 2008
14 SCP 10

FOR THE NEWEST MEMBERS OF THE FAMILY,

ETHAN AND SADIE

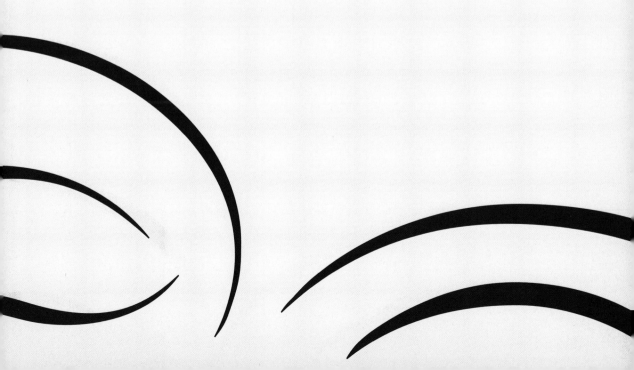

CONTENTS

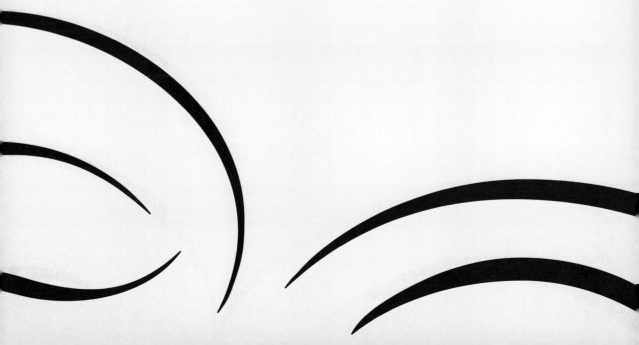

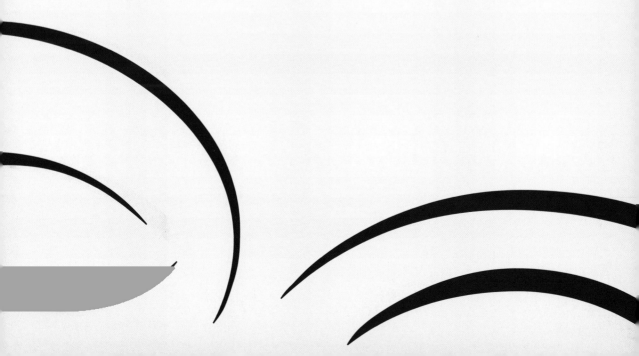

I HAVE BEEN A FICTION WRITER BY CHOICE AND INSTINCT for a long professional life. It has been a leap for me to tell the truth.

In a delightful way, nonfiction is easier to write. The plot and characters are already served up, as joyful as breakfast in bed. But nonfiction has a harrowing downside. I could not invent new scenes or punch up old ones. As I was six years old when Houdini died, I couldn't ring him up to pin down some elusive detail. I was boxed in by the recorded past. I was unable to pluck Houdini's conversations out of thin air. If he didn't say something, neither could I—or not without first warning the reader that a brief exchange was a bit of ventriloquism across the decades. You may see my lips move on a page here and there.

I did not trip over the Houdini story by accident. During my callow youth, I transformed myself into a professional magician and came to know Madame Houdini in her last years. While I eventually escaped into the world of writing, I bring a magician's special sensibilities to Houdini's world.

In sleuthing the escape artist's life, I had the benefit of two good friends, skilled magicians and scholars both, who were renewable sources of enthusiasm and encouragement for all things Houdini. I offer my profound gratitude to David Avadon and Tom Conley. They kept me honest.

CHAPTER ONE
HE WAS BORN, BUT WHERE?

NOT LONG AGO THE BREAST POCKET SNIPPED from a man's pajamas came up for auction in New York City. Immediately, bids around the room erupted like doves flushed from cover. So eager was the crowd for this fragment of sleepwear that a lofty price of $3,910 was reached before the auctioneer banged his hammer and shouted, "Sold!"

Why would anyone want the pocket of an old pair of striped pajamas with the initials **HH** monogrammed in gray?

Easy. The first initial stood for Harry. The second for Houdini.

Harry Houdini, the world's greatest magician and escape artist. No jail cell, no chains, no manacles could hold the man.

Houdini, who walked through a red-brick wall! He came through without a scratch, too.

Houdini, who clapped his hands like cymbals and made a five-ton Asian elephant disappear into thin air. Not even the elephant knew how he did it.

Like those engaged in the ancient commerce in relics of saints, buying and selling a wrist bone here, a great toe there, today's magic collectors seek anything associated with the supernova of sorcery, the incomparable, the fabled Houdini—even a trivial scrap of flannel.

This powerfully built but diminutive young man was the most commanding wizard to burst upon the world scene since Merlin performed his parlor tricks during the misty days of King Arthur. Houdini could have sawed Merlin in half.

An abject failure as a magician in his early twenties, Houdini woke one morning, like the poet Lord Byron, to find himself famous.

A knockabout kid, the son of an impoverished rabbi, he insisted that he was born in Appleton, Wisconsin. An ambitious finger flinger, he crowned himself King of Cards, with holes in his socks. Leaping onto a carousel horse at full gallop, he reached for the gold ring of stardom—and caught it. That, perhaps, was his greatest sleight-of-hand trick, as we shall see.

What exactly did he do that so excited the world's imagination? What razzle-dazzle fixed the name Houdini in the public memory so firmly that it is still remembered today, more than eighty years after his final disappearing act?

Watch him.

Tightly strapped and buckled into a canvas straitjacket designed to restrain the violently insane, he is being raised by his ankles to dangle like a fish from the cornice of a tall building. He wriggles free as adroitly as a moth emerges from a cocoon. The crowd cheers. Can nothing hold the great escape artist?

After recrowning himself the "King of Handcuffs," a defiant Houdini is being shackled at the wrists and ankles. He is quickly nailed inside a wooden packing case and thrown into the untidy waters of New York Harbor. Moments later, he splashes to the surface, rattling aloft the police jewelry.

He has escaped the inescapable. The skeptics are befuddled. The man must have supernatural powers!

Equally confounding is his trademark Indian Needle Trick.

Apparently swallowing thread and 100 to 150 sewing needles, he extracts the needles from his lips to dangle and flash in the spotlight—each one threaded! Impossible!

Was the devil at work here? Does it need to be said that anyone who lacks the secret of trying to thread needles with the tonsils had better first make a reservation at the nearest emergency room? As a devout magician, I am able to reveal only that I may *not* reveal Houdini's secrets.

Just as nature abhors a vacuum, a gap in the logical mind needs to be filled. Forgetting that magic tricks are designed to defy logic, the dumbfounded rush in with nonsensical explanations to plug the vacuum. As Houdini's fame expanded, so did the absurdities.

If Houdini wasn't in league with Old Splitfoot, perhaps he could shrink himself like a cheap suit of clothes, to allow chains and handcuffs to drop off. Even better, maybe he could dematerialize himself like so much fog to slip through the bars of a jail. So insisted Sir Arthur Conan Doyle, author of the Sherlock Holmes stories.

These "exposés" were harmless enough, and Houdini must have smiled to himself, for he knew how his tricks were *really* done.

Houdini doing what he did best—laughing at restraints.

At the same time, the faux secrets were demeaning, for they dismissed the magician's hard-won sleight-of-hand skills and mastery of the arts of fooling the socks off people. Houdini was the grand guru of magic. He didn't need the unseen assistance of sprites, spirits, and imps.

It is said that you know you are truly famous when the deranged imagine that they are you.

Once Houdini's exploits blazed across newspaper headlines, the opportunists, the cunning, the nutcases, and the jealous emerged like theatrical chameleons. The imitators not only parted their hair in the middle, as did the escape artist, they mimicked his style of dress and his billing. There were more self-crowned Kings of Handcuffs before the footlights than in all the royal houses of Europe—half a hundred in England alone. To Harry's great annoyance, these pests tried to counterfeit his name, coming up with such worshipful thefts as Whodini, Oudini, and Hardini.

Women, too, tried to get into the act. Most nettlesome was a Miss Undina in Germany whose name, when pronounced, sounded close to the original. He had to sue to get her and her copycat tricks out of the escape business. And where a heavily manacled Houdini had had himself photographed in his under-wear, an imitator named Miss Lincoln had herself photographed in a racy costume that could pass as knee-length bloomers. But not even the curves and black stockings of that distaff queen of handcuffs were a match for Harry's commanding footlight razzmatazz.

His strategy was to trump his imitators with ever more daring and death-defying feats of mystification. It was this battle for supremacy that inspired one of his most dangerous illusions—the awesome Milk Can Escape.

In earlier days, milk fresh from the cow was transported in large cans. Houdini had one made just large enough to hold him tightly folded in a fetal position. Buckets of water were poured into the can, followed by Houdini himself. Challenging his audience to hold its breath with him, the great showman lowered his head under water. The lid was secured with six padlocks, and a curtain was drawn around this impending death scene.

At thirty seconds the audience was gasping for breath. Sixty seconds passed. *Tick, tick, tick.* Two minutes! Had the escape gone wrong? *Tick, tick, tick.* Was Houdini drowning?

Assistants with axes stood ready to burst open the death can. At the last moment, just short of 180 seconds, out popped the master of escape, breathless, dripping wet, but very much alive.

HE JESTS AT HANDCUFFS shouted a Los Angeles newspaper, while Houdini challenged the world to duplicate his escapes. But as the years passed, he could read his voluminous scrapbooks, and they were telling him that flinging off handcuffs was no longer making headlines.

While his name had become as recognizable as that of Napoleon, of Shakespeare, of Lincoln, the former carnival magician feared slipping back into obscurity. He understood that fame needed constant renewal, and he went at it with ingenuity and furious energy.

He took up flying in a canvas airplane that looked like a box kite. He became the first aviator to conquer the air in Australia. This not only made headlines, it put him in the history books.

He became a movie star, using his skills at sleight of hand and escape to foil the villains. In one film scene, he frees himself from barbed wire! In another he is weighted with a ball and chain and thrown into water. He lives to tell about it.

Houdini in Winnipeg, Canada, about to escape from a tightly strapped straitjacket. A penciled note on the back of this photo says that the temperature was flirting around thirty degrees below zero.

Houdini, once a bottom-of-the-playbill vaudeville performer, rose quickly to the top. Here he is in the 1920s, on a bill with Spanish dancers. One of the Cansinos would grow up to become the movie star Rita Hayworth.

For a long time he had been cocking a skeptical eye at the trendy public embrace of Spiritualism. This hoax busied itself within dark chat rooms where the believers attempted to talk to the dead.

But the ghosts had quirky ways of communicating. Sometimes they made rapping sounds to spell out their messages. They might lift heavy tables to let believers know they were on the premises. That must have been quite a feat for a ghost with no more substance than a warm breeze. At other times the spectral voices would come pouring forth from brass trumpets. They even came whistling out of the spouts of teakettles! The real wonder is that these magic stunts were taken seriously. Didn't the innocents know that talking trumpets and teakettles could be bought at any conjuring shop? And why would the dear departed resort to such daffy goings-on?

Houdini immediately launched a crusade to expose the bald-faced trickeries. The spirit mediums who were fleecing the gullible fought back, of course, but once again Houdini was in the headlines. He nested there, the most talked-about American in America, until his sudden death on Halloween night in 1926.

The cosmic whimsy of that night of the goblins couldn't have been lost on him during his final hours. He'd come so far in a short life from those humble beginnings in Appleton, Wisconsin. If, indeed, that's where he was born.

Harry, you pulled a trick on us. That's not where you were born.

Some snoop dug up your birth certificate. The masquerade is over.

CHAPTER TWO
FROM RAGS TO RAGS

WHEN I WAS A YOUNG SLEIGHT-OF-HAND MAN traveling with a magic show, I found myself in Appleton, Wisconsin. Appleton! The Midwestern Taj Mahal of the magic world. The birthplace of the incomparable Harry.

He had set my fancies and ambitions aflame when I read of Ehrich Weiss's rags-to-rags childhood here amid the shady elm trees of Appleton. The red-backed book, written by a newspaperman named Harold Kellock, launched a thousand young magicians like me. Its pages set down scripture on the life of the great conjuror. I virtually knew the text by heart.

Houdini was a cobbled-together name. Just as his biography inspired my generation of magicians, Ehrich's dreams had been excited by an earlier life story of an earlier wonder worker, Jean Eugène Robert-Houdin. The great French prestidigitator had modernized magic in the mid-nineteenth century by trashing the commonly worn astrological robes and rag-pickers' garments of vagabond conjurors. Robert-Houdin presented himself as a gentleman in formal dress. He took magic off the streets into the best theaters.

But it was the romance and adventure in his larger-than-life memoir that heated Ehrich's imagination. As a teenager, he quickly light-fingered the great Frenchman's name for himself.

He was to explain, "A fellow player, professing a veneer of culture, told me that if I would add the letter I to Houdin's name, it would mean, in the French language, 'like Houdin.'"

And so on that faulty premise, the deed was done. Since Ehrich was called Ehrie at home, it was the small change of a vowel and the addition of a consonant that produced "Harry."

"Can you tell me where I can find the Houdini house?" I asked a large, straw-haired policeman on sidewalk patrol.

The officer gave a shrug. Was he expected to know trivia like that?

In his Appleton years, young Ehrich Weiss is dressed in a many-buttoned coat that must have been as formidable to escape as straitjackets would be in his Houdini years to come.

Houdini's scholarly father, Rabbi Mayer Samuel Weiss, whose passion for books was passed on to his vagabond son. The escape king traveled with a special bookcase jammed with a hundred books, so that he'd never be without reading matter.

I added, "Houdini was born here in Appleton, you know."

His eyebrows lifted slightly. "You sure?"

Sure? Positive! It was right there in Kellock's thick, red-backed book.

"Well, it's sure news to me," the cop said and moved on.

I was stunned and a little pained. He didn't know. That was like being unaware that Moses had briefly resided among the bulrushes.

Unburdened by local history the patrolman may have been, but my ignorance was superior to his ignorance. Houdini was nowhere to be found in the environs of Appleton on March 24, 1874, the day he was born. That great event, his first escape into a disinterested world, happened in the Jewish ghetto of Budapest, Hungary.

A former soapmaker, his father was university educated, dignified, and bespectacled Rabbi Mayer Samuel Weiss. Initials trailed his name like an academic pigtail: Ph.D., L.L.D.—formidable degrees entitling him to the title of doctor. He was master of several languages. He wrote poetry. He excelled at everything but making a living.

In the late 1870s a rumor spread throughout Europe that the streets of America were paved with gold. Dr. Weiss sailed to New York only to discover, like other immigrants rushing ashore, that the streets were common mud and worthless cobbles.

It took Dr. Weiss two years to scrape together enough money to send for his wife, Cecilia, and their four sons, one of them the future bamboozler. After a fearful fifteen-day voyage, the eager family joined him in a Midwestern town of seven thousand called Appleton. The small Jewish community of fifteen families had hired Dr. Weiss as the first resident rabbi, at two dollars a day.

It didn't take the good rabbi long to discover that he was still dirt poor and hardly able to feed his ever-enlarging family.

As I rambled about the town half a century later, I could imagine a kid shining shoes on the corner I was approaching or peddling newspapers on another. Now I wonder if Ehrich shouted the headlines in Hungarian-inflected English, an accent some fellow magicians later said never completely disappeared. At any rate, his earned pennies and nickels helped keep the Weiss ménage afloat.

Ehrich was developing into a lithe but muscular kid. He taught himself to be an acrobat and contortionist, skills that would prove essential later in his career as a "self-liberator," a billing he sometimes assumed.

He claimed to have begun his professional career at age seven in Appleton, but better authorities say he started at nine in Milwaukee. He pulled on long red woolen stockings to make his public debut in a backyard five-cent circus. Billed as Eric, the Prince of Air, he pronounced himself "the star performer."

Prince? That was his first leap into the ranks of royalty. With an ever-busy ego, the ermine robe of monarchy beckoned him, and in due time he crowned himself king. King of Cards.

Recalling his brief experience with the nickel circus, he claimed to have hung from a trapeze while picking up needles with his eyelids!

Should one believe this? Of course. Did it actually happen? Of course not. It was the sort of hype and backstory that great heroes assume to enrich their legends.

What the Prince of Air truly did while hanging from the trapeze was pick up pins with his teeth. It was an applause getter, but any trapeze artist could do the stunt. With his vaulting fame Houdini chose wisely to escape from the common herd and to present himself as unique. So the pin story underwent spicing up, with a touch of bamboozle.

Despite the family's foundering existence, Harry in later life looked back on his Appleton years with great affection. There his parents had spent "the happiest years of their lives," he wrote. In England, on a rented typewriter, he remarked to his brother Dash, "I actually dreampt of Appleton Wisc a short time back and beheld Pa and Ma drinking coffee under the trees in that park . . . and chatting as they did when you and I were romping kids."

As suddenly as a snap of the fingers, Appleton vanished from young Ehrich's life. Dr. Weiss, unable to speak English, was let go. The congregation had lost patience with his Old World services conducted in German. They wanted a New World rabbi who spoke English.

Dr. Weiss moved his family to nearby Milwaukee, where his talent for failure flourished. The Milwaukee years were misfortune wrapped in hard times inside a calamity. Looking back with unconcealed pain years later, Houdini wrote, "The less said on the matter the better."

To ease a burden on his parents, Ehrich ran away from home.

He was twelve years old.

Chapter Three
KING OF THE NECKTIE CUTTERS

EHRICH YEARNED TO EARN ENOUGH MONEY TO SEND a few dollars home. He hopped a freight train he thought was bound for Galveston, Texas, but his sense of direction was faulty. The train was going to Kansas City, Missouri.

He had clumsily planned his first great escape, this one from home. He'd brought neither food nor spare clothing. When he hit the road out of Kansas City, there were no roads to speak of. These were horse-and-buggy days, and he followed wagon ruts wherever they might lead. He came to a village named Delavan and discovered that he was back in Wisconsin. Running away wasn't as easy as he had imagined.

Hungry and tired, so one version of the runaway saga goes, he knocked at a door to ask if there was some work he could do in exchange for a meal. Road kids were nothing new to motherly Mrs. Flitcroft, and she didn't resist this weary, black-haired ragamuffin.

She dusted him off and fed him. She gave him a place to sleep and sewed up a rip in his trousers.

He scratched out a postcard to his mother, saying, "I'm going to Galveston, Texas and will be home in about a year." The post-card still exists. Anticipating his place in the sun, Houdini never scrapped anything with his name on it.

He remained with the Flitcrofts all winter, earning extra money to send home by shining shoes and selling papers in town. Eventually receiving a letter from his mother, Ehrich learned that his father had gone to New York in a desperate attempt to change his luck.

The runaway headed east, slowly working his way to New York and a reunion with his father. He never forgot Mrs. Flitcroft, and he sent her significant gifts for the rest of her life.

Working as a New York department-store messenger boy, Ehrich pooled his savings with his father's elusive fees as a Hebrew teacher. They sent for the rest of the family waiting in Milwaukee.

Even as a raw youth, Harry sensed the value of self-promotion. He had himself photographed in the full regalia of a messenger boy. At age thirteen, he was earnestly helping to support his family.

If it seems that Houdini had been running all his life, he now began to run for sport. He joined the Pastime Athletic Club on the East River at 67th Street. He was fast. He won sprints. Soon athletic medals, "most all real," clung like leeches to his tank-top running shirt. A sportswriter declared him to be "the greatest swamp runner" ever to slog his way across the boggy northern end of Central Park.

His choice of sports was, after all, limited. Baseball and basketball were so new they were little more than a rumor. Football was just beginning to cross the ocean and make its sea change from the baffling game of British rugby.

One can see in these early triumphs his determination to excel at any endeavor. For the rest of his life, he regarded being second best as a punishment.

At the same time, he was discovering the world of magic.

While only informal surveys have been taken, it appears that most magic buffs date their strange infatuation to the gift of a toy-store magic set when they were boys. Others were enchanted by witnessing a conjuror pull coins out of their ears.

Neither seems to have been the case with Houdini. Finding himself sitting in a darkened theater and feeling bedazzled by a wonder

Adorned here with a chest full of running medals, Houdini
soon began to regard himself as a magician.

worker certainly plowed the ground for magic to take root. While still in Wisconsin, he witnessed a performance of an English illusionist, Dr. Lynn, who was making himself famous by chopping off an assistant's limbs. At least the conjuror had the grace to slap the employee back together and get off a few laugh lines. Why audiences will flock to see a woman sawed in half or a man dismembered is for Dr. Freud to explain.

Houdini wrote of seeing the performance, being transfixed, but he didn't rush out to buy a rabbit to pull out of his cap.

That had to wait for New York. He got a job as a cutter in a necktie factory, where he met an older kid, Jacob Hayman, who was an amateur magician. With his dark, neatly trimmed mustache and center-parted hair as polished as his shoes, Hayman even looked like a magician. Ehrich did not.

Like most boys, Ehrich had picked up a magic stunt or two. Unlike most boys, who master a secret or two and move on, his fascination with tricks took hold. Why mystifying your friends fixes itself as a lifelong passion with only one in thousands has never been probed.

But there's abundant evidence that conjuring attracts unpopular minorities. Jews, among others, figure largely in the history of magic, from Moses with his snake trick, to Herrmann the Great, whose mustache and goatee set the style for conjurors, and on to Houdini and David Copperfield.

Give a magic wand to a high-school kid who feels invisible, who can't get a date, and—voilà!—he is empowered and transformed. (As part of my magic persona in school, I used to read palms, which is pure bunk, but it gave me a chance to hold a girl's hands.) Mastery of sleight of hand is a great equalizer for the outsider, the disadvantaged, and the short.

Ehrich was a perfect fit. He was an immigrant, he was poor, his religion was unpopular, and he was short.

His modest stature haunted him for his entire adult life. In a passport document issued in 1900, he gave his height as 5'4". Behold! He began to grow like Pinocchio's nose. A few months later, in follow-up documents, he rose to 5'6" and finally to a towering 5'7".

There survives a photograph of Harry standing beside a big fellow, a magician and fellow royal, T. Nelson Downs, the King of Koins. Houdini can be seen rising to his toes for the camera.

Upon his meeting Jacob Hayman in H. Richter's Son necktie

Two monarchs. The King of Koins (T. Nelson Downs) and the King of Handcuffs appear to be the same height. Look more closely and you will see that Houdini has done a trick with his toes.

factory on Broadway, Ehrich's conjuring skills expanded. But the epiphany, the life-changing event, was waiting for him in a bookstall.

There, for a dime or so, he picked up a battered copy of the now classic autobiography of a great French magician, *The Memoirs of Robert-Houdin, Ambassador, Author and Conjuror.*

He had been struck by lightning. His own biography would strike later generations with the same voltage. Here was adventure and derring-do! Here was magic! Robert-Houdin had triumphed over poverty and obstacles much like Ehrich's own.

"From the moment that I began to study the art, he became my guide and hero," Houdini wrote of the French master. "I accepted his writings as my text-book and my gospel. What Blackstone is to the struggling lawyer . . . or Bismarck's life and writings to the coming statesman, Robert-Houdin's books were to me."

And then he added, without suspecting that he would later attempt to expose the Frenchman as a hoaxer: "I asked nothing more of life than to become in my profession 'like Robert-Houdin.' "

Exit Ehrich. Enter Harry Houdini.

Chapter Four
THE PYGMALION OF EAST 69TH STREET

It's a stretch to believe that Houdini ever thought of himself as a modern Pygmalion, the mythical Greek sculptor who created a woman out of ivory—and promptly fell in love with her. But peering at the unshaped raw material of his being, Houdini was moved to pick up a chisel and set to work. He carved in his brand-new name.

He chiseled a false birth date, claiming April 6 for the great event. It was only decades after his death that the actual date was discovered to be March 24. His astrological sign, Aries, remained unchanged, but that could hardly have mattered to him. His withering disdain for the junk sciences—astrology, tea-leaf reading, palmistry—was right up there with his contempt for Spiritualism and its chattering ghosts, as we shall see.

Now that Houdini had begun his sculpture, it would become a lifelong work in progress.

And like the Greek before him, he would fall in love with it.

The kid with the scorned Jewish name was swept away in the sculptor's rubble. It was an escape from delusional anti-Semitism, as common then as the runny nose. The national pastime of gnashing one's teeth at the Irish, the Jews, the Italians, and the Catholics was a social impulse even more tolerated than chewing plug tobacco and spitting on the floor.

It seems clear that Houdini, still living in obscurity at 305 East 69th Street, would allow nothing to distract him from his perceived destiny. But if he meant to keep his Jewish self under wraps, he did a haphazard job of it. Once successful, he would set up and preside over a beneficial theatrical association for the sons of rabbis like himself. Members were such Broadway stars of the day as Al Jolson and songwriter Irving Berlin.

Forming a theatrical partnership with his fellow necktie cutter Jacob Hayman, he began giving magic shows around the city. They billed themselves as the Brothers Houdini.

This is regarded as the earliest photograph of Houdini as a magician. As is typical of brand-new conjurors, he appears to have on display every magic prop he owns. He is nineteen years old.

The enterprise was a risky means of support, but Harry quit his job as a necktie cutter. It was sink or swim, and he was already a strong swimmer. He'd figured out that only practice would lift his skills out of the ordinary. He began to practice card and coin sleights four to five hours a day.

The world barely noticed the Brothers Houdini. With only an occasional booking, the act found itself on a treadmill to nowhere. The entertainers were reduced to playing low dives and beer halls for "throw money"—small change pitched into a hat. Hayman quit and went back to work at the more profitable necktie trade. Eventually he would become a Baptist minister.

Retaining the Houdini stage name, Harry had no shortage of brothers to fill out the billing. He collared his younger brother, Theodore, whom everyone called Dash, to work as his assistant.

A showstopping masterpiece was already waiting half polished among Houdini's few props. Earlier, he had persuaded Dash to loan him his life savings, some sixteen dollars, with which to buy magician's equipment from a retired wonder worker. The haul included a well-scuffed trunk.

The trunk looked ordinary enough and could be examined, but it had been cleverly rigged to allow anyone locked inside to escape and reappear from the back of the theater. The trick had had a great success in England, where it originated, but it had failed to excite much notice when adapted and performed by the Brothers Houdini.

Houdini had already learned a few escape secrets. Contrary to what the public believed, he knew that any set of handcuffs could be opened with the same key. And a friend had introduced him to the ancient art of rope trickery. He was becoming expert at slipping out of restraints.

Houdini now took a fresh look at the prop trunk and saw a more powerful way to present it. He combined his escape skills into a quick-change illusion he called Metamorphosis. It was an inspiration.

Here's what an audience now saw. Houdini stood with his wrists knotted behind him in a spiderweb of ropes. A bag was pulled over his head like a sausage casing and the top tied off.

The magician was then stuffed inside the trunk, which was quickly bound with stout ropes and heavily padlocked.

Dash, a tall, husky teenager in bow tie and knee-length pants, then stood ready to close the curtains of a small cabinet around the trunk. "When I clap my hands three times—behold a miracle!" he shouted.

He stepped behind the curtains and did the count. One . . . two . . . *three!* The curtains parted and *behold*, indeed! There stood young Houdini, escaped from trunk, sack, and ropes!

The trunk was unwrapped and unlocked. The mouth of the sack was quickly unknotted. Out popped Dash, now bound with his wrists behind him, as Houdini had been, in the spiderweb of ropes.

"Metamorphosis!" shouted Houdini in his commanding tenor voice.

In time, this baffling blink-of-an-eye escape and double change would become one of Houdini's signature tricks. Later he would add an additional restraint: Handcuffs were locked around his wrists. For these tryouts, audiences sat amused but unmoved. The trick didn't lay an egg, but why didn't it hatch? Houdini speeded up the quick change. It was tightened to three seconds!

Success remained elusive. What was wrong?

According to legend, Houdini's speech was right off the streets of New York. He was a dees, dem, and dose magician. His verb of choice was ain't. "I ain't got nothing up my sleeve."

When a theatrical friend pointed out his lowbrow grammar, Houdini characteristically rose to the challenge. He went to work on his speech.

Was it his clumsy grammar that had cast a gloom over the escape illusion? Apparently not, for he was never again caught saying "ain't" in public, but it didn't matter.

It's easy to imagine how mystified Houdini must have been that the trunk trick was failing to make him famous. Perhaps the answer lay in a newspaper account of an audience that was too stunned to react and applaud. It happens.

The substitution, or sub trunk, as magicians today call the truly remarkable illusion, is still everywhere performed. I am not alone in regarding it as one of the two or three most beautiful mysteries ever staged—and perhaps the most fascinating of them all. I have twice worked in the trunk trick with traveling shows. In the first we didn't have money to buy a sub trunk and made the flash change from a canvas sack. In the second, after a minor road accident, I found myself truly locked inside the badly shaken trunk. In repairing the trunk, the show manager had nailed the escape hatch shut! Not even the great Houdini himself could have slipped out.

When as a young teenager I first read of the illusion that Harry named Metamorphosis, I didn't know what the cursed word meant. I wondered how Houdini, with hardly enough formal education to read words of more than one syllable, had come up with such an obscure and freakish word.

I had forgotten that he grew up in a house stuffed with books and alive with learning, impoverished as it may have been. "My father had reared me in the love of books," he wrote. Later, as a show-business headliner, he traveled with a specially built bookcase stuffed with a hundred or so books.

Houdini had learned to educate himself. He never took a magic lesson. He was an autodidact—one who teaches himself. He trained himself in the difficult card sleights he needed. While never tested, he brought to each succeeding challenge an I.Q. that must have been lofty.

Not only was he reading any texts on magic he could lay hands on, he collected books, as had his father. In something more than a decade he would reveal himself to be an author, a publisher, and an editor of the most prestigious magazine for magicians. His work is still read today. Eventually he would leave to the Library

At age twenty, Ehrich Weiss dressed for success as The Great Houdini. At first a theatrical nobody, he credited Beatrice—called Bess—with bringing him luck.

Waiting in the wings was Wilhelmina Beatrice Rahner, who was to marry Houdini after a courtship of two weeks. This picture was taken soon after the wedding. She was eighteen.

of Congress the finest collection of magic books and playbills ever assembled.

If there was anything right about the Brothers Houdini failing act, it was Harry's smile. The performances may have seemed commonplace, but not that boy-next-door smile. You could feel it across the footlights.

The young magician was eighteen, and turning handsome. Then his father died. Almost as suddenly, he got married.

Chapter Five
Dressing Up the Act

ON HIS DEATHBED, RABBI WEISS ASKED HIS MAGICIAN son to assume the responsibility of caring for his mother, Cecilia. The scene has the solid ring of myth.

Why would the dying man lay the responsibility on a son living a down-at-the-heels existence from his handcuff escapes and card tricks? What kind of career was this? And didn't the rabbi have two older, more promising sons?

Still, Houdini wrote that as his father lay dying, he called "me to his side and made me repeat the promise that my mother would never want for anything."

Houdini's lifelong devotion to his mother was extreme and exclusive. In one family photograph of Harry with his wife and seated mother, he appears to be an only son. A younger brother, Leo, who was to become a doctor, had been standing in the picture. Poor Leo was retouched out of existence. This was not to be Houdini's only embrace of the retoucher's art. As we shall see, he vanished whole unwanted crowds out of pictures in order to spotlight himself exclusively.

It's quite possible that his father gathered all of the Weiss children at his side to make the same request. But the famous deathbed promise has the appearance of a self-serving obligation, providing Houdini with a stamp of approval for his extraordinary and obsessive devotion.

It was the same devotion and Old World chivalry that he lavished for a lifetime on Bess, a Brooklyn girl whom he was to meet in 1894 and two weeks later, marry. He had just turned twenty.

She was part of a heavily lipsticked song-and-dance act that called itself The Floral Sisters. Harry immediately bought out his brother Dash and put Bess in the magic act. The Brothers Houdini were quick-changed into The Houdinis.

Dash took his walking papers with characteristic good grace. He developed his own magic and escape act.

Eighteen-year-old Wilhelmina Beatrice Rahner—that is to say, Bess—was a sprite, a petite Roman Catholic girl with lips dimpled at the corners (much like Houdini's own) and large soulful eyes. Evidently, Cecilia Weiss thought the magician son of hers could do no wrong, and she accepted Bess with an Old World embrace. The bride's mother, on the other hand, had a seizure. When she learned that her daughter had provided her with a Jewish son-in-law, she cut Bess off without another word.

The fit lasted for twelve years. Finally, when she discovered to her astonishment that Houdini did not smell of brimstone and have horns and a tail, the two families united. Bess was then a worldly woman of thirty.

Nevertheless, after Houdini left her house, Mrs. Rahner would sprinkle holy water about—just in case.

With such a brief courtship, the couple was in for some surprises. Bess discovered that her husband slept only five hours a day. Houdini discovered that his wife's pretty head was stuffed with fearful Dark Age superstitions. She believed, among other folk fancies, in "ghosts, witches, and the power of the evil eye and lived in constant dread of supernatural evils." Believers were convinced that someone possessing the evil eye could, with a mere glance, zap you with bad luck. Houdini set about to pluck the superstitious notions from her head.

This anticipated his later passion to unmask as theatrical trickery a trendy, superstitious cult of the day. Calling itself Spiritualism, its self-anointed priests of the dead seemed able to summon gossipy ghosts from the great beyond into neighborhood living-room séances. Houdini's exposés rivaled his uncanny escapes as headline grabbers.

Bess quickly abandoned her homegrown superstitions but got back at her husband.

Said she, "He boldly preserved certain little taboos of his own. For instance, he, who was ordinarily without fear, and deliberately risked his life in dangerous public exhibitions week after week for many years, would take no risks whatever on Friday the thirteenth. On that day he would cut out all hazardous acts from his stage show and would perform no outdoor feats."

Take that, Harry.

Needless to say, Bess dressed up the shabby magic act. The trunk trick took on added charm when a pretty girl in long white

The newly married Houdinis—Bess is eighteen, Harry twenty.
They had met only a couple of weeks before and remained devoted
until Houdini's dramatic death thirty-two years later.

The Houdinis ate well during their circus years. That's Harry in the
starched collar and Bess in the bow tie. But where's the fat lady?

An early showcard featuring Harry as the circus magician—before he discovered that escape was where the money was hiding.

tights delivered the mantra. "Ladies and gentlemen, when I clap my hands three times—behold a miracle!"

And three seconds later, out popped Houdini—night after night, in rough dives, beer joints, and storefront sideshows that called themselves dime museums.

Houdini always credited Bess with changing his luck. "Shortly after our marriage," he wrote, "hard times struck us good and plenty. A great many actors were out of work. But, she has been my luck. I never had any before I met her, and it has been with me ever since."

At this time, Houdini had not yet chipped out Budapest as his birthplace or begun to carve in Appleton. In fact, he occasionally billed himself as the Hungarian Magician and later, with Bess, as the European Illusionists.

Their luck *did* change. And a notable vaudeville theater booking popped up when their youthful energy caught the eye of a top-hatted showman with a theater he'd named after himself. With a twist of his waxed mustache, the impresario hired them for a week as opening act in the famous and trendy Tony Pastor Fourteenth Street Theater! In New York before the turn of the last century, this was the top of the show-biz ladder.

Houdini could hardly show up at Tony Pastor's in his thread-bare, battle-worn tuxedo. When this came to the attention of two lifelong friends, Hattie and Minnie Mooser, the sisters produced an immaculate tuxedo with a snap of their fingers. Their brother Leon, a theatrical manager just in from Shanghai, wouldn't be needing his formal dress that week.

Looking classy and confident in the expensive tux, Houdini made his big-time debut. Vaudeville was the popular television of its day. It was an escape from the tenements for performers with a flash of talent. Hitting it big was being struck by lightning, but it happened.

The opening act on any vaudeville show was reserved for the weakest performer, and that's where the Houdinis stood in the theatrical pecking order. But in was in.

Houdini had not called himself the King of Cards for nothing. He did his most accomplished card flourishes. Then, as the King of Handcuffs, he shook himself out of knotted ropes and clanging manacles. When the high-speed Metamorphosis illusion reached its stunning climax, the audience went wild. Perspiring, smiling, on top of the world, he reached for Bess's hand as they took a bow.

With a wave of his heavily ringed hand, Tony Pastor moved the

Houdinis up to fourth spot on the bill. They were no longer an opening act.

The closing place was reserved for Maggie Cline, an Irish singing star of the day. She stopped Bess outside her dressing room and asked, "My God, child, who made you up?"

Bess admitted sheepishly that she was her own makeup artist.

"Come in here, kid." The older woman smiled. "Let me fix you." In her dressing room she plastered cold cream on Bess's face and gave her a quick and skilled makeover.

When Houdini next saw his wife, he had to give her a second look. Was that Bess? He fell in love all over again, as he was to do throughout the years of their marriage.

The Houdinis closed at the end of the week, returned the borrowed tux, and waited for offers to come flocking in. After all, the great Tony Pastor had written them a note putting his okay on their act.

But hard times trumped even Tony Pastor's smile. The Houdinis found themselves at liberty again except for an occasional small-time gig. In his pocket diary Harry wrote, "Missed train. Had to walk 8 miles with heavy grip in rain."

Finally came an offer from Lancaster, Pennsylvania, to join the Welsh Brothers circus at "twenty-five dollars a week and cakes." That is to say, a place to sleep and all they could eat.

It was a comedown from Pastor's. As Bess wrote, "We arrived in a night of drenching rain with a howling gale and stumbled about in ankle-deep mud for miles in the dark, trying to find the [circus] tent. . . . At last a voice in the darkness hailed us . . . and the next instant we were pulled into what looked like great black cave. It was the [sleeping] car—an old truck."

Their compartment was closed off from the other circus acts by a flimsy curtain and a cardboard partition. The furnishing included only a cot, for the room had no space for such luxuries as a chair or table. Whatever makeup was left on Bess's face must have run off. "Still soaking wet, dismayed at the strange environment, the darkness, the cramped quarters, I fell on the cot sobbing." That was to be their home for the next twelve weeks.

While he had comforted her, Houdini seemed untroubled. The next morning he was up early, refreshed and ready to start performing. They were to work the sideshow and the main show, doing magic, doing Punch and Judy puppets, doing mind-reading, doing song and dance, doing the trunk trick, doing the circus parade, and anything else the boss, Mr. Welsh, could think of for them to do.

There were no animals in the circus, but one thing Mr. Welsh did want to stage was a Wild Man act. He had a ferocious Wild Man of Java banner he had accumulated that was going to waste.

Houdini was game. Rigging up clothing out of gunnysacks, messing his dark, curly hair, and applying red stripes down his cheeks, he rattled the bars of an old wooden cage. The ringmaster pointed his malacca cane and in the tradition of sideshow barkers played the English language as tunefully as if it were a calliope. Something like this:

"Ladies and gentlemen, avert your eyes if you are under age or are given to faints and vapors. Ladies, smelling salt will be provided if requested. But to the bold and daring among you I direct your gaze upon this genuine flesh-eating, lip-smacking cannibal from the deepest and wildest jungles of Java—the real thing! An untamed, hot-tempered, snorting, growling WILD MAN! He terrorized the countryside before he was captured. He has the bite of a crocodile and no table manners to speak of! He's a WILD MAN!

He dines on raw meat, cigarettes, and cigars. Watch your hands, sonny! Don't get too close or you'll have to point with your elbow!"

The ringmaster threw Houdini a raw steak to gnaw on. Men in the audience would pitch cigars and cigarettes to hear the Java Wild Man growl. (As Houdini didn't use tobacco, he gave the circus men free smokes later.) The act was a smash hit and stayed in the show.

The magician's first jailbreak is an oft-told story. It may have occurred when the circus paused to put on its show in a small town near Providence, Rhode Island. It was a bad day for circuses—Sunday. Blue laws dictated that no entertainment be staged on the Sabbath, and the entire troupe was thrown into jail.

Show business understands the value of a good myth. I have no doubt that the circus troupe was thrown into the clink, but I have trouble with the rest of the drama: Miserable in her tight cell, the fat lady bursts into sobs. Houdini, ever chivalrous, breaks into action. Waiting until the sheriff is gone, the magician borrows a hairpin from Bess. He picks the lock of the cell door and lets the fat lady out. He also frees the other performers.

Houdini's inspired and powerful idea to use jailbreaks as publicity stunts is presumed to have arisen from this bucolic adventure. I would love to believe it. But is the myth a bit too neat? And that charming photograph of the Houdinis with their fellow circus performers—there's a missing person who betrays the fable.

Where is the fat lady?

Sometime later, farther north in St. John's, Nova Scotia, the magician visited an asylum for the insane and saw a straitjacket for the first time. He wondered how he might escape from all those restraining straps and buckles. He bought one to practice with.

He now had all the props he would use to make himself famous.

THE YEARS 1896 AND 1897 WERE YEARS THAT TRIED
a magician's soul. Everything Houdini touched turned to
ashes. Bookings largely eluded him. Stranded in St. Louis in the
dead of winter, living in an unheated hotel room at $1.50 a week,
hungry, Harry and Bess stole several potatoes. Finding an old
wooden crate, they broke it up and built a small fire in the small
clunker of a cookstove. They feasted on roasted potatoes.

How curious, then, that he noted in his diary for October 11,
1897, that he'd lost $60 shooting craps. Really? Couldn't he resist
conning his own diary? Playing the high roller? The sum was vast for
its day, representing far more than a month's salary. In today's cash,
$60 expands to $600 or $800. This, at a time when the wolf was

yapping at the Houdini door—and they didn't even possess a door.

So what would Harry be doing walking around with a bankroll big enough to stuff a turkey? It appears that Houdini's impulse toward braggadocio began early.

Booking prospects were no better in New York when the Houdinis reached home. For the first time in his life, Houdini gave way to despair. He went to the leading newspapers, offering to sell the closely held secrets of his act for twenty dollars!

The editors showed no interest in running such an exposé. Who had ever heard of Houdini and his handcuffs and trick trunk?

As Professor Harry Houdini, he opened a school of conjuring at 221 East 69th Street. He offered to teach, as well, how to make ghosts walk and other tricks of the Spiritualists. They were skills Houdini had been dabbling with for some years but had not yet found a use for in the act.

The academy of magic proved hardly more successful than his father's Hebrew school.

Finally an offer turned up for a fifteen-week run in the show-business boondocks—a traveling medicine show in Kansas.

Houdini found it easier to escape this padlocked milk can and create a sensation than to free himself from the punishing luck of the mid-1890s, which created such gloomy prospects that he wanted to throw in the theatrical towel.

Harry and Bess scratched up train fare, loaded their trunks, and hurried west.

Traveling under the impressive banner of Dr. Hill's California Concert Company, two impressive men of medicine, both quacks, pitched their magic elixir on street corners. They offered their tonic as a miracle cure for everything from appendicitis to flat feet. The miracle would have been if the potion cured anything.

The performing Houdinis attracted the tip—the crowd—and helped to sell the bottled bunkum. Later, at the local opera house, they'd join other performers in an evening performance. Tickets went for ten, twenty, or thirty cents. Often they were a tougher sell than the whiskey-spiked elixir.

It was here that the Houdinis found themselves working with comic knockabouts Joe and Myra Keaton. Among other acrobatic tricks, they would throw their limber two-year-old son about the stage like a rag doll. One day the kid accidentally tumbled down the high backstage stairs to be caught unhurt by Houdini, who happened to be standing below. The magician turned to reassure the boy's parents. "That's some buster your kid took."

That's how Buster Keaton got his stage name. He grew up to

become a great comedy star in silent movies, right up there with Charlie Chaplin.

The medicine show went bust in Galena, Kansas. Spiritualism being the rage even in the sticks, Houdini offered to read minds and make ghosts walk on Sunday night in the opera house. It would keep the theater company afloat.

The problem wasn't that the séance wasn't good enough—it was *too* good. Earlier in the day, Houdini had visited the cemetery and taken notes on the dead. He conferred with a local gossip and with a few rumpled greenbacks bought the man's silence.

The theater that night sold out. The small towners were swinging from the chandeliers. When Houdini conjured back the musty dead, he addressed them by nicknames and drew forth dark family gossip. The locals sat stunned. Some rushed into tears.

When the séance ended, while taking his bow, Houdini could see that raising ghosts paid off better than shucking handcuffs. Listen to those hands clapping!

The Houdinis followed the Galena success with a part-time career as ghost wranglers and mind-reading fakers. Members of the audience were often invited to write personal questions on slips of paper, which were then folded and collected. Without seeming to unfold the billets, Houdini would clasp one to his forehead. Aided by psychic powers, he'd call out the question and improvise an answer from the dead—from his earlier crib notes.

Don't be deceived. The only power Houdini possessed was a magician's ability to cheat the billet open without being detected and to glance at the question.

Or he might wrap a piece of chalk between two school slates and—*scratch, scratch, scratch*—the spirits would grasp the chalk and scratch out advice to the griefstricken. Trick slates or switched slates, the methods were commonplace to insiders.

It didn't take many months before his father's dead hand reached up and grabbed Houdini by the ear. "Ehrich, what are you doing? The son of a rabbi making a business from the sorrows of others?"

Houdini was shaken. What *was* he doing? Pouncing on the ease with which decent but naive people abandoned common sense to accept his parlor trick as supernatural? He was exploiting them. While he hungered for glory, his conscience now put the Houdinis out of the spirit business.

Never again did he stage a ghost show as if it were genuine.

Houdini caught onto the secret of fame. All you needed to do was get your name in the papers.

He kept walking into newspaper offices to announce, "I'm Harry Houdini, the King of Handcuffs! I can get out of anything."

And the replies often went like this: "Splendid. Let's see you get out of my office!"

Big-city editors wouldn't send reporters to cover this twenty-four-year-old pesky kid. His handcuffs were fixed, weren't they?

Quite accidentally, toward the end of 1898, Houdini made a huge discovery. It was a word—a power word, complete with exclamation point.

Challenge!

He had attracted small-town publicity with his jailbreaks. Now he'd try it in a big city—Chicago. On the inspiration of the moment, he flung out the power word.

He challenged the police to shackle him in the department's own cuffs and turn the key on the cell door. Nothing could hold the King of Handcuffs! Watch him saunter out, moments later, a free man!

The police took the bait. No one clamped in Chicago's iron manacles was going to walk out of a Chicago jail as if it had rubber doors. The event would be news, and the papers sent around reporters.

Houdini was out before the reporters finished their cigarettes. He was prepared for an ovation.

But the escape king's glory was snatched from him. Reporters learned that he had had a look at the cell the day before and had probably made wax impressions of the locks.

Houdini folded his arms defiantly. "Suppose you strip me and search me before you lock me up?"

It was done. His mouth was sealed with plaster so that he could not hide keys inside. Stark naked, he was again locked up and his clothing placed out of reach in another locked cell.

In a party mood, the police and newspapermen waited in the chief's office. Their ears were cocked for a muffled wail for help.

Instead Houdini walked in on the party, jaunty, smiling, and fully dressed.

The story was rushed to the city's presses. Embracing Bess later, he shouted, "Success! Success!"

And then the newspapers hit the streets.

"Bess! Bess! I'm famous!"

CHAPTER SEVEN
MR. BECK BECKONS

Houdini's sudden fame was written in vanishing ink. Filling out an engagement at a Chicago dime museum, Houdini saw a husky detective come forward. He was accepting the handcuff king's challenge and snapped a mean pair of manacles on him. "Let's see you get out of those!"

Houdini immediately recognized the irons as regulation cuffs. They'd be easy to beat. He had a passkey.

Behind a screen, he got down to business. He sleight-of-handed the key from its hiding place and put it to work. The cuffs balked. They refused to jerk open. The bolt wouldn't budge.

Houdini was bewildered. Wrong key? Impossible! Sweating now, he continued his kingly labors. Time passed, and the restless audience began jeering at him. After an hour, the hall had emptied. He was still struggling with the police bracelets.

Finally the detective took pity on him. "Do you give up, Houdini?"

Houdini was resolute. "No."

"Well, I might as well tell you. I poured in birdshot to jam the works. Those cuffs ain't never going to open again. You'll have to be sawed out!"

The defeat made the gleeful newspapers. They liked a good joke. The King of Handcuffs had been dethroned! Instead of a scepter, the Wizard of Shackles ought to be holding jester's bells.

With his onion-thin skin, Houdini was profoundly wounded. Imagine having to stand while someone sawed off the cuffs! The humiliation! His abundant ego was assaulted. Bess tried to comfort him, but it was useless. He convinced himself that his future had been snatched away!

"I'm done for," he told Bess. "We might as well quit."

But they still had a booking in Minneapolis to fill. Bess was glad to get him out of town and away from the scene of his public disgrace.

The Chicago joke had reached Minneapolis ahead of them. Houdini would never again allow a pair of handcuffs to be snapped on him without first making sure they hadn't been doctored.

One night, a portly, well-dressed stranger remained after the performance. Speaking in a soft voice, with the sputter of a German accent, he invited the Houdinis out for a bite to eat and to discuss an offer.

Once seated, the older man told Houdini that their act was a disaster. It lacked focus. But perhaps something could be done with it. Why not retire those moth-eaten magic tricks with silk handkerchiefs and playing cards? The act might have a future if it were presto-changoed around its big numbers, the challenge handcuff escape and the breathtaking trunk trick.

Who is this wise guy? Houdini must have wondered, until he looked again at the man's card.

He was Martin Beck.

The Martin Beck! Everyone in show business knew the name. The Houdinis were sitting across the table from one of the

You are not seeing double. That's Harry "Handcuff" Houdini, as he sometimes called himself, on the left, about to shuck off half a dozen police cuffs. The clone is his devoted younger brother Dash. Harry taught him the act.

most powerful men in the trade. He booked for the Orpheum circuit of theaters. This was big time. And Mr. Beck was beckoning. He had a hunch that he had found a diamond in the rough. "I'll try you out on the circuit at sixty dollars, and if you make it go, I'll raise you."

Sixty dollars *a week*. In those days, when you could buy a loaf of bread for three cents, Beck was talking big money.

The next thing the Houdinis knew, and to the envy of their fellow vaudevillians, they were on the train west with Martin Beck in their hip pocket. They would open in San Francisco. It was June, the last year of the century: 1899.

Vaudeville had become the hit form of family entertainment, presenting eight or more novelty acts, and changing the bill each week. The vast theaters, with their plush private boxes, had risen as the new cathedrals of the city. There, families gathered in weekly reverence to sit in the darkness. They sat awed by the marvels of the acrobats and jugglers, the world-class singers and comedians.

Vaudeville was a galaxy vast light-years away from roughneck beer halls and dime museums. The Houdinis had been accustomed to a daily grind of ten to twenty performances a day. In San Francisco, vaudeville demanded only two. This was class. This was big time.

Unlike Svengali, who used hypnotism to create a great singing star in George du Maurier's novel *Trilby*, Martin Beck used only his personal charm and vision. Acting on the theater man's advice, Houdini abdicated his crown as the King of Cards, though he kept a deck in his hip pocket for emergencies. He mothballed the sucker die box, a classic comedy with a die that vanishes from a box and reappears in a hat. He junked the borrowed watch trick, the timepiece crushed and restored from a shot with a blunderbuss pistol. He found a new home for the doves.

When Houdini reached the Golden Gate he had re-created himself as a three-trick magician—Indian needle swallowing, handcuffs, and the sub trunk. Each was dynamite.

Within days, he shook San Francisco like an earthquake.

The police there had never before heard of an escape artist. And they'd never been so recklessly challenged. After they stripped and searched Houdini, they locked ten pairs of handcuffs on the "rash young man." So heavy were the manacles around his ankles that he could barely hobble into the jail cell. He had as much iron on him as a junkyard.

He was out like a jackrabbit and leaped into the headlines. He became a West Coast sensation. It was here that he introduced his trademark escape from a straitjacket. Martin Beck, waiting in the East, got the theater reports. He advanced the Houdinis' salary to ninety dollars a week. It was a bedazzling sum.

Houdini recovered his old confidence and optimism. His one-man publicity machine went into overtime. He took out an advertisement in a magicians' journal that seems to be the first public appearance of a slumbering ego beginning to erupt. He modestly asked, "WHO CREATED THE BIGGEST SENSATION IN CALIFORNIA SINCE THE DISCOVERY OF GOLD IN 1849?" Could the answer be Prof. H. Houdini, as he signed himself?

This was not the first time Harry had assumed academic standing. Magicians commonly used the puffery of calling themselves professor, even if they were close to illiterate. But one senses that it pleased Harry to have the cachet of a professional title. Like his father's.

Houdini repeated his jailbreak in Los Angeles, and Martin Beck fattened his salary to $125 a week. Harry bought Bess a fur neckpiece and continued sending money home to his mother for family expenses.

Now the New York Svengali advised Bess and the handcuff king to pack their trunks. The Houdinis needed to catch a steamship and storm Europe, where escape artistry would be fresh. They could then return to the United States in triumph and humble New York for having scorned them in the past.

Eventually, going to Europe turned out to be a brilliant career move, as Beck had foreseen. And it was in London that Houdini took up the chisel and again chipped away at his self-portrait.

There, on August 9, 1900, Houdini was obliged to fill out a passport application in the American embassy. And there came the familiar line "I solemnly swear that I was born at . . ."

One wonders how long Houdini hesitated before scratching in "Appleton," in the state of Wisconsin?

At that moment, the Budapest immigrant vanished. In his place stood Houdini, a native-born Yankee Doodle! A by-gosh American!

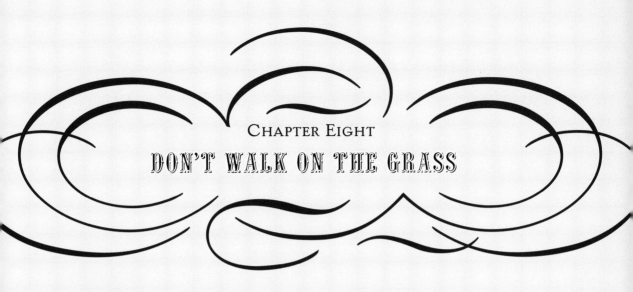

CHAPTER EIGHT
DON'T WALK ON THE GRASS

HOUDINI WAS SUPPOSED TO PLAY LONDON'S ALHAMBRA Theatre, in all its Moorish splendor, but he was thrown out before he could open. The manager had never heard of him and had no record of the booking. Furthermore, an American magician calling himself the White Mahatma had hit London with handcuff tricks some years before without setting the place on fire.

The red carpet Houdini had been expecting had been yanked out, jerking him into a pratfall. Houdini's incandescent temper burst into flames, and he turned on Martin Beck. Already smoldering about the fifteen-percent commission he had to pay his manager, Houdini erupted over the mishandling of his London debut.

Forgetting that Beck had plucked him like a drowning cat from obscurity and coolie wages, Houdini fired his portly and pince-nezed adviser. He'd manage his own affairs. Beck went on to a new triumph. He built the great Palace Theater in New York that became the dream booking of every vaudevillian.

Houdini had to have felt a moment's concern about following in the stumbling footsteps of other American performers whose acts had failed to thaw British reserve and had evidently burned up the territory. And Houdini knew that his old friend Samri Baldwin, who billed himself as the White Mahatma, was a powerful magician whose handcuff mystifications had inspired Houdini's own shackle act. Still, wasn't Houdini raising the art of escape to new heights?

His ambitious eye had not strayed from the glorious Alhambra, the show-biz mecca of London. The manager agreed that if this brash American could escape from Scotland Yard manacles, he'd book him into the Alhambra.

Houdini ate challenges for breakfast. "Can you go with me now?" he asked.

They hurried over to the police, where Scotland Yard men had Houdini wrap his arms around a pillar. The officers slapped several pairs of handcuffs on the self-crowned escape king.

These weren't stage handcuffs, the police superintendent pointed out with an air of confidence. They were the Yard's strongest. "Well, here's how we fasten the Yankee criminals who come over here and get into trouble," he added, and started for the door. "I'll come back for you in a couple of hours."

What happened next is legendary.

"Wait!" cried Houdini. "I'll go with you. Here's the way the Yankees open the handcuffs."

The escape king walked away from the pillar, leaving the manacles in a junk heap on the floor.

It's a question whether anyone, even Houdini, could spring open so many cuffs so quickly. The usual explanation is that Houdini, with his vast knowledge of locks, knew of a fault in the design of English cuffs. One could crack them open with a sharp blow to a precise spot.

Somehow, escape Houdini did, and he found himself on the stage of the Alhambra at £60 a week. Say, $300. Say, more than ten times that in today's money.

The news of his besting of Scotland Yard swept through

Houdini looks you straight in the eye and vanishes five passengers! On a return to the United States, the magician found himself aboard ship with former president Theodore Roosevelt. Not one to share the spotlight, he had other passengers doctored out of the photograph.

London like a north wind. Houdini was an overnight sensation. He was famous all over again.

His contract with the Alhambra was renewed and renewed once more. He was thrilling audiences, puzzling them, entertaining them, and above all, night after night, selling out the house. He was held over at the Alhambra for six months.

A headliner playing in London at the same time, Houdini's old friend from America, the King of Koins, jangled a full ring of keys. "Houdini, here are the tools you do your act with," said T. Nelson Downs, laughing.

Houdini seemed insulted. "Tom, I don't use keys."

"Well," replied the coin king, "you can't open them with hot air."

Meanwhile, theater managers from all over Europe got word of the American phenomenon and sent telegrams seeking to grab the handcuff king for their theaters.

He needed someone to sort through the chaos. Shrugging off his recent disloyalty to Martin Beck, he hired a London agent, Harry Day, to manage his theatrical affairs. Day immediately booked him into a theater in Dresden, Germany.

Houdini must have turned seasick green in advance of the trip.

Although a strong swimmer, he had become so acutely motion sick on the steamship from New York that in his delirium he threatened to end his misery by jumping overboard. Bess had kept him tied to his bunk with bedsheets, with the knots underneath so that he couldn't escape.

Now he would have to cross the notoriously rough English Channel. His pallor when he staggered ashore in France can be imagined. He bounced back, of course, lugging his ever-expanding press books and with a daring new publicity stunt in mind. His ego, too, was ever expanding. As one wag put it, Houdini declined to walk on water only because of his fear of seasickness.

In Dresden, while weighed down with chains and manacles, he proposed to leap off a local bridge into the river. It would be a dramatic but dangerous stunt.

The Dresden police said no.

Houdini made the death-defying jump anyway one September day in 1900. Bess couldn't watch. He had long practiced holding his breath in the bathtub for longer and longer periods of time. Now, with breath to spare, he stayed underwater until the anxious crowd watching from both riverbanks must have thought he had joined the fishes. When Houdini finally burst to the surface, laughing, free of manacles and chains, the crowd went wild.

Houdini had touched a live wire. He was a man who seemed able to escape the shackles of daily existence. In Germany, this had a special appeal. The master of escape excited the dream of triumph over the rigid Teutonic culture of strict rules, "where everything not compulsory was verboten." The onlookers cheered inwardly and outwardly for this American who snapped his fingers at the fetters of life.

But when Houdini, dripping wet, crawled onto the grass, he was arrested. There was no law forbidding a cheeky blockhead from leaping into the river, but there was a law forbidding him to walk on the grass.

Houdini was fined a handful of German pfennigs.

Pennies. The newspaper notoriety was worth millions.

The escapist piled sensation upon sensation and headline upon headline. By the time he moved on to Berlin, theater managers were fighting over him. This might have spun the head of any actor.

Despite the show-biz warning not to believe one's press notices, Houdini appears to have believed everything he read. After so many years of grinding poverty with no more visibility than a lightning bug, he was ready for acclaim and fortune. His bumptious ego now had something to be bumptious about.

He became arrogant, self-worshipful, and demanding. In the words of the poet Robert Browning, he had "an itch for the praise of fools." His conceit was expanding like a supernova.

Great and gifted men are, after all, human. They commonly harbor flaws and weaknesses of character. Daniel Defoe, author of *Robinson Crusoe,* despised children. The German opera composer Richard Wagner was a sputtering anti-Semite. Napoleon had a nasty habit of invading other countries. French poet François Villon was a thief. Houdini was cocky.

His cockiness outraged some of his fellow magicians, and his success excited their professional jealousy. A cottage industry was born, devoted to shooting down the monster. The trashing thrives to this day.

When Houdini had signed the passport document at the American embassy, he swore to return to the United States in two years. He missed by whole calendars.

The handcuff king reigned in Europe for four and a half years.

CHAPTER NINE
THE QUEEN'S DRESS

HOUDINI KEPT LEAPING OFF BRIDGES WITH THE GUSTO of a seal. He filled theaters to standing room only. He seemed the biggest thing to hit town since the Ice Age. Germans went "escape crazy."

He was becoming a legend at the age of twenty-seven.

But ants had come to his theatrical picnic. Houdini's epic success brought with it pest life that persisted throughout his career—if it wasn't the copycat Houdinis, it was others eager for their fifteen minutes of fame. His newfound enemies tried to shoot down the great mystifier by exposing his methods.

In London, a stranger leaped onto the stage of the Alhambra Theatre and denounced Houdini as a fraud and an imposter.

The U.S. Postal Service put its stamp of approval on Harry Houdini in 2002. He adapted his name from Jean Eugène Robert-Houdin, whom the French immortalized with a postage stamp in 1971. Harry would no doubt have preferred that his stamp be larger than that of the magician he regarded as a liar, a thief, and—even worse—an inept magician.

The two women in Houdini's life—his mother, Cecilia Steiner Weiss, and Bess, whose mother threw her out for marrying a Jew. Mrs. Weiss took her in.

"I am the original handcuff king!" he proclaimed. Then he added the coup de grâce. "And you're not an American, sir! You've never been to the United States!"

Before Houdini could reply, a man in the audience stood up. "That is not true," he said. "I also am an American, and I saw him several years ago doing his handcuff act."

The audience burst into applause. Houdini whispered to Bess to get the Bean Giant handcuffs. "We'll fix this fellow now."

The Bean Giant was a massive and cunning manacle invented in Boston by a Captain Bean. Even its own key wouldn't open it— without being fitted with a special extension.

After demonstrating, behind a curtain, that he could escape from the Bean Giant, Houdini snapped the irons on his accuser. "And here, sir, is the key."

You can be sure this was the key lacking the extension piece. The stranger struggled and sweated and swore under his breath. Finally he had to beg Houdini to release him. A roar of laughter greeted the challenger. The audience gave Houdini an ovation.

A year or so later in Cologne, he was again accused of fraud by a German police official named Graff. He claimed that Houdini could not escape from any manacles, as advertised, but only from his own presumably doctored ones. That was a deception on the public, he insisted.

Houdini dragged the policeman into court for slander and proved him to be mistaken. Graff appealed the verdict, eventually arguing the case before the highest German court.

To decide the case, the justice led Houdini to a heavy steel safe in his office. He said, in effect, "If you can open that, I will make my decision."

Houdini was left alone, and this was his time to break into a sweat. While in Germany he had apprenticed himself to a locksmith in order to master the entire range of German locks. But he had not counted on safe work.

He stared at the infernal box. It could easily sink his career. He glared at all that intimidating steel. He had no idea where to begin to crack the safe. He gave the handle a furious yank. The door swung wide open.

The safe had been left unlocked.

Houdini must have had to restrain himself from bursting out laughing. How lucky could one get?

To make his safecracking look like serious work, he kept the justice waiting. Finally calling him in and showing the safe wide open, Houdini captured fresh headlines across Germany. The handcuff king had performed the impossible. He'd beaten the *Polizei* in court.

Earning huge sums, Houdini was able to send for his mother, so she could revisit Europe for the first time in more than twenty years.

A strange bit of luck turned up. In a London shop window, a dress with a high neck and fur cuffs caught his eye. It had been sewn for Queen Victoria, who had died earlier that year, 1901. It was for sale.

He saw that the gown was about his mother's size. In a theatrical gesture of mother love, he presented it to Mrs. Weiss for a homecoming reception in Budapest. She allowed her picture to be taken in it, but one doubts that the humble woman ever wore the pretentious and quirky gift again.

Meanwhile, imitators continued to plague Houdini. Theater owners had discovered that escape artists were money in the bank and they hired anyone who could break out of a paper sack.

Houdini countered by sponsoring a rival of his own. He cabled his brother Dash: "Come over. The apples are ripe."

Houdini not only designed the new act—modeling it after his own and booking it—he chose a professional name for his young brother. Dash became Hardeen. Once Hardeen was turned loose on Europe, in a seven-year success, an imitator quickly turned up, snatching both names in a single grab. He called himself Hardini!

Success filled Houdini's pockets with excess English pounds and German marks. He could now afford to haunt Europe's bookstores in search of anything relating to magic. He began to collect with a magpie's passion that was unmatched in the world of conjuring. In addition to old books, he built up a collection of broadsides, playbills, and other theatrical paper. He was preserving historical trivia that would certainly have disappeared.

He had in mind to write an ambitious encyclopedia of magicians. Doing that would enable him to pay homage to the French hero of his hungry youth, Jean Eugène Robert-Houdin.

The last month of 1901 found the Houdinis in Paris. While always immaculately dressed on stage, Houdini was as indifferent to his rumpled offstage attire as General U. S. Grant. But on this occasion, for this homage, he put on his finest suit. Bess knotted a new cravat. He boarded a train for the small town of Blois, some four hours away, and there he bought a great wreath to lay on the grave of Robert-Houdin.

But Robert-Houdin's daughter-in-law refused to come to the door. A sculptor, she had never heard of an American mystifier named Houdini and couldn't be bothered.

However injured Houdini's feelings may have been, he laid the locally bought, elaborate wreath on the French magician's tomb and, hat in hand, bowed his head "for fully half an hour."

At the same time, the reception he had received from the Houdin family—for this was his second attempt to meet with them—must have begun the chill that was soon to replace his moony worship.

By the time he finally sat down to do his book, some seven years later, the homage had turned itself inside out. The idea for a vast encyclopedia was largely abandoned, though he was to write the detailed entry on magic for the *Encyclopaedia Britannica*.

His new and angry focus became *The Unmasking of Robert-Houdin*. The great American magician had determined that the great French magician was a liar, thief, and fraud.

CHAPTER TEN
THE SIBERIAN MYSTERY

IN 1903, HOUDINI POPPED UP IN MOSCOW, WHICH was a magic trick in itself. No foreign Jews were allowed into Russia. With the full approval of Czar Nicholas II, the Russian cavalry was set loose to terrorize and murder Russian Jews in the infamous pogroms (today we use the term *ethnic cleansing*). It was a dress rehearsal for the copycat Nazi madness that swept through Germany thirty years later.

How Houdini strode across the border into Russia can only be guessed at. Bess, a Catholic, had filled out the paperwork, and she may have converted Harry on the spot. A Moscow showman had seen Houdini perform in Paris and had offered him a bushel of rubles to "please" fill the man's theater.

The magician was never one to let a good public prop go by without embracing it. In Holland, he had had himself chained to the blade of a windmill. If he had failed to escape, it was only because the blade had broken with his added weight. When a dead sea monster washed ashore off Cape Cod in 1911, he was sewn up in it. Although the noxious fumes almost finished him off, as I will explain later, he escaped first.

In Moscow, it was a notorious Siberian prison van that caught his magician's eye. Drawn by horses, it was a huge steel safe with a zinc floor, used to transport prisoners on a cruel, nonstop three-week journey to their frozen exile. No one had ever given the van the slip; it was regarded as escape proof.

How could Houdini resist? He was stripped naked, thoroughly searched for tools, and locked in. After struggling for half an hour, the sweaty escape artist came to the small window and asked the sentry to allow him to talk to Bess. As she gave him a final kiss, she was roughly hustled away. Then Harry returned to his labors.

He got out of there.

Of course! He didn't call himself the Self-Liberator for nothing. How he pulled off this escape has left magicians arguing to this day. No one quite believes the widespread notion that Bess passed him a tiny saw and can opener as she gave him that quick forbidden kiss—the can opener to split open the zinc floor. A more convincing possibility was put forth decades later by a Houdini buff: "Look, it was Holy Russia, wasn't it? The easiest way out of the prison van would be with a hundred-ruble note inserted in the right place—the pocket of the jailer."

Would Houdini pull off a cheap trick like that? Certainly. To a magician, effect makes the world go round. Effect is muscle. How he flexes it is nobody's business.

When Houdini made his final escape from Russia, he and Bess felt an immense sense of relief. As a Jew, he had thumbed his nose at the bloodthirsty Cossacks. The magician chose never to return.

Back in England, a humorless weight lifter from Blackburn, a city in the northwest, was waiting to trip Harry up and, quite likely, end his career. He meant to grab Houdini's standing reward of £25 (a tidy sum in today's dollars) to anyone who could so restrain the handcuff king that he was unable to free himself.

The challenge had packed the theater. The challenger, whose name was Hodgson, stepped before the footlights with six pairs of heavy handcuffs, chains, and padlocks. By then, Houdini was familiar with every manacle afloat in England, France, and Germany. He had lost no sleep over Russian irons—the workmanship was so shoddy that it took little more than a friendly rap, he claimed, and cuffs would oblige by springing wide open.

Houdini saw at once that there was something wrong with Hodgson's handcuffs. The areas around the keyholes were badly scratched. He recalled the incident in Chicago when a challenger had jamed the cuffs with birdshot.

The Blackburn conversation is easy to imagine.

"Mr. Hodgson, you won't mind if we test these cuffs before I put them on."

"Mr. Houdini, I do mind. Your claim is that you can escape from any cuffs. Kindly put them on, my dear chap."

"My dear chap, I'd be a fool to kindly put them on. These have been tampered with."

"You forfeit the twenty-five pounds?"

"In a pig's eye!"

By this time the audience had turned against Houdini. A deal was a deal, and the charge of tampering sounded like an excuse.

Sensing hostility, Houdini reluctantly agreed. Now the audience applauded. It had come to be entertained.

Hodgson went to work. He put Houdini in a ton of leg irons and snapped on the handcuffs. Then, with his bulging muscles, Hodgson wrapped chains around the magician, trussing him up in a kneeling position.

A cloth cabinet was placed around Houdini, who was left to struggle unseen. The theater orchestra began to play. After fifteen or twenty minutes, Houdini called for the cabinet to be removed. He had far from escaped—he had fallen to his side and couldn't get up. He asked to be helped to a vertical position. Hodgson refused.

The cabinet, or ghost house as Houdini called it, was replaced. The orchestra resumed. Houdini recalled, "My back was aching, my circulation was stopped in my wrists, and my arms became paralyzed. I suffered so under the strain that I asked to be let out." His arms, in fact, were turning blue, and he wanted the chains loosened only long enough to get his circulation back.

Hodgson refused. "This is a bet. Cry quits or keep on."

Now the audience turned against Hodgson.

Again, Houdini went into seclusion.

Houdini's smallest advertisements beat the drums at the highest volume. Here he challenges members of the audience to bring along their own hardware.

Iconic photograph of the young handcuff king wearing more police jewelry than clothes.

Almost two hours later he reappeared from the ghost house. His clothing was ripped, his arms were bleeding. He heaved the chains and manacles at Hodgson's feet, saying, in effect, "Now, go to hell, sir, you muscle-bound nuisance."

Not much of the audience was left, but those who remained burst into wild applause. Hats sailed into the air. Umbrellas, too. Houdini found himself facing a standing ovation. The smiling American was invincible!

He had to be. He hadn't struggled to save the £25. He had just saved The Great Houdini from defeat and oblivion. The trapdoor of failure was always underfoot, waiting for Ehrich Weiss.

Bess seemed anxious to go home. It had been years! And Houdini clearly felt that the time had come for his assault on New York.

But before packing his trunks for the dreaded sea voyage back to the States in 1904, Houdini got trapped. A challenge that he couldn't duck had been flung at him.

In London, the *Daily Illustrated Mirror* had gotten hold of an ugly pair of handcuffs that had taken a locksmith some five years to design and figure out. These cuffs "no mortal man could pick," the locksmith assured the newspaper. "They were Houdini-proof."

Gloating in advance, the newspaper flung out the challenge: Let's see the Self-Liberator get out of *this* steel trap.

It was a challenge Houdini was too professional to dismiss. New York could wait. And since a newspaper was involved, he could count on enough print coverage to consume an entire pine forest. The London Hippodrome would sell out within hours.

It did. At three o'clock in the afternoon, some four thousand Londoners showed up for the historic contest. The event had the air and anticipation of a bullfight.

"I am ready," announced the monarch of manacles.

Ovation.

A newspaperman snapped the cuffs around Houdini's wrists and then "turned the key six times, thus securing the bolt as firmly as possible."

Houdini looked worried but retired to his ghost house. The orchestra played. And played. And played on.

Some thirty-five minutes later, Houdini emerged, still hand-cuffed. His collar had broken open, sweat was running down his face, and there was a pained look on his face.

"My knees hurt," he explained.

Out of a sense of humanity, the newspaper provided a cushion. The royal escapist ducked back out of sight.

Another twenty minutes of concert music. Houdini was back.

"Will you remove the handcuffs for a moment?" he asked. "In order that I may take my coat off?"

The newspaper people conferred. Fearing some sort of trick, the reporter replied, "I am indeed sorry to disoblige you, Mr. Houdini, but I cannot unlock those cuffs unless you admit you're defeated."

Houdini declined that invitation. Able to reach a penknife, he cut himself out of his coat. The audience cheered. They knew savoir faire when they saw it. For five minutes their yells filled the theater.

Bess, standing in the wings, had become so tense and anxious that she had to leave the theater.

Ten minutes later, The Great Houdini stepped through the curtains—free! He displayed the handcuffs with their claws wide open, like dead lobsters.

Reported the *Mirror*, "A mighty roar of gladness went up. Men waved their hats, shook hands one with the other. Ladies waved their handkerchiefs, and the committee . . . shouldered Houdini, and bore him in triumph around the arena."

Not only was his reputation for invincibility secured, Houdini was becoming the sort of hero that myths are made of.

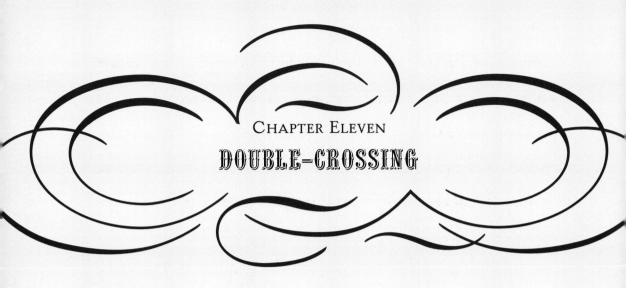

CHAPTER ELEVEN
DOUBLE-CROSSING

WHEN BESS MARRIED HARRY SHE WAS EIGHTEEN years old, with a limited view of the vaudevillian's life that lay in wait for her. She would become a bird of passage. Even after they became successful, she was obliged to nest in boardinghouses and hotel rooms. She lived out of steamer trunks. Ten vagabond years had passed without a kitchen or bathroom of her own, or a wall to hang a picture on.

But for Harry the return to New York was a disappointment. His former manager, Martin Beck, had promised brass bands to greet them as they stepped ashore from their triumphs across the pond. Not a piccolo was to be heard.

Great European stars they were, but the New York theater

managers were only half impressed and offered only half the salary the Houdinis had commanded abroad.

They soon headed back to London. But not before Bess got a kitchen of her own. They bought a brownstone house at 278 West 113th Street—a cozy little abode of four stories, with more rooms than they needed. Harry finally had a place for his huge and exploding collection of magic books and show-business memorabilia. He astonished himself. "Am havin[g] an awful time with the books I brought back," he wrote. "Never realized the amount, until I tried to get them into my home."

And at last he could whisk his mother and siblings from the family hovel on 69th Street to a residence of distinction.

At home in the British Isles again, Houdini perfected stage tricks he'd been tinkering with for years. In Glasgow he accepted a challenge to make his escape from a stoutly reinforced straitjacket—it took him a cliff-hanging fifty-five minutes. Well, maybe.

One can't be sure.

He had learned that the longer he took to liberate himself, the more anguished on his behalf the audience became. When he finally burst free, the thunder of applause would rattle eardrums.

ESCAPE! The Story of The Great Houdini

A rumor arose in the magic world that he would routinely make his escapes in a few minutes and then read the newspaper or play solitaire for twenty minutes or so. Only then would he muss himself up and pop through the ghost house curtains and face the audience.

This was showmanship. Even his professional enemies, and he had flocks of them, conceded that as a showman the world had not seen his like before.

He was now spotlighting the Indian Needle-Swallowing Trick. He was by no means the first to claim to thread needles with his epiglottis. He'd gotten the secret in his dime-museum days from a carnival geek who called himself Maxey, the Human Sewing Machine. The stunt can be traced back to the early 1800s.

Magicians are aware that audiences are repelled when things are brought forth from the mouth. Houdini nevertheless lifted the trick out of the show-business gutter. Dressed in evening clothes, he gave the mystery style and humor. "You'll notice that I dine on the needles *eyes* first, so they can see on the way down."

The trick is widely performed today, but only one or two performers have made of needle swallowing the showstopper it became for Houdini.

He was to advise his fellow conjurors on the difference between doing a trick and presenting a trick. "The reason magicians do not forge to the front more than they now do, is because they content themselves with a mere doing . . . [as if] all they have to do is lay the apparatus on the table and go from one trick to the other."

For a trick that became one of his headline grabbers, he'd have loose lumber waiting on the stage and invite a committee of men to join him. He'd hand each volunteer a screwdriver. Before the eyes of the world they'd construct a packing box, driving long screws in all the way. Sometimes he'd use nails instead, for the apprehensive *bang bang* of hammering.

Certainly no one was going to escape from that infernal pine box. No one but the incomparable Great Houdini, who'd pop out like a jack-in-the-box.

By this time, his London manager was able to get Houdini not a weekly salary but an unprecedented slice of the box office receipts. He was now pulling down well over $2,000 a week—a tsunami of currency in 1904, tax-free money.

Houdini appears to have swallowed needles, and now pulls them out fully threaded. Don't try it without first arranging for a tombstone. The trick's a trick.

Wrapped like a pot roast, Houdini is about to make an underwater escape.

He had no intentions of ever returning to the States, except to retire to his Manhattan home. He felt that he'd been treated like an opening act, not the headliner that he was so clearly was. The big theater-chain bookers would have to get on their knees and "beg to get Houdini."

They did. A cable arrived from New York, offering a now respectable $5,000 a week. He had the satisfaction of cabling back to say that he was completely booked, as indeed he was.

When the fall of 1905 came along, with princely cables still on the table, the Houdinis made the seasick crossing again. They moved into their own home in New York at last, and Bess had a bedroom of her own to fix up, to say nothing of fourteen closets.

The following year, she became seriously ill. She wanted to see her estranged mother. Fearless Harry, who thought nothing of jumping off bridges, must have gulped inwardly at having to confront his combative mother-in-law.

Nevertheless, he hopped over to Mrs. Rahner's apartment and swore that unless she put on her hat and accompanied him back to Bess, he wouldn't budge from her living room. That prospect must have shaken her, for she ran for her hat.

Both bursting into tears, Bess and her mother reconciled. Twelve years were enough! Mrs. Rahner, mother of eleven, even became proud of her son-in-law, The Great Houdini. She would eventually move into the town house on West 113th Street and accept his support.

Chapter Twelve
THE INK-STAINED WRETCH

NOW THAT HE WAS BACK ON HIS HOME SOIL, IT WAS time to kick up some dust. He quickly made an art of jailbreaking and, in fact, advertised himself as Harry Houdini the Jail Breaker.

He launched a great buzz when he arranged to be locked up in Cell No. 2 on Murderers' Row of the South Wing of the United States Jail in Washington, D.C. What was so special about Cell No. 2? It was not only that the narrow door stood recessed deeply into the massive brick wall. It was not only that the lock had been installed around the corner, out of reach—some three feet away. It was that a famous assassin had been a resident of the cell for a year and been unable to slip away. He was bewhiskered Charles Guiteau, who has gone down in history as the man who shot and killed President James A. Garfield in 1881.

Houdini was stripped naked and searched. His clothing was locked in another empty cell. Then he was left alone, except for the eight prisoners languishing in their cells along Murderers' Row.

Wrote the warden, "Mr. Houdini, in about two minutes, managed to escape from the cell and then broke into the cell in which his clothing was locked up."

At that point in his escape, Houdini "was seized with a whimsical idea." When he returned to the warden's office, now fully dressed, he said, "I let all of your prisoners out." If the warden were given to heart attacks, he would have had one then. Before he could sound the alarm, Houdini added, "But I locked them all in again." Indeed he had—in different cells!

For the next three years, Houdini made jailbreaks a regular feature of his appearances in Boston and other cities on the Keith chain of theaters. When he strode into town, he was no longer just an entertainer. Houdini was an event.

But the itch for ink and authorship had gotten hold of him. When his first book was published in 1906, he signed himself with a double-barreled salute: HARRY HOUDINI, Handcuff

King and Jail Breaker. He bestowed upon the work a tantalizing title: *The Right Way to Do Wrong*.

This ninety-six–page book was a retelling of stories of cunning swindles and underworld lore he'd picked up in police stations during his world travels. You'd learn, for example, not to expect to be burglarized under a full moon. Housebreakers sought the darkness of the new moon.

He exposed the method used by a gang of chewing-gum jewel thieves in London. Their secret was to dispatch a gum-chewing woman to shop for gems. She'd manage to stick one under the counter with a wad of spearmint. After the jewel was discovered missing, the woman was searched but had to be released. Later, other members of the gang would return on a shopping trip and retrieve the stolen gem.

They were caught, of course, as if to prove that thieves can't steal and chew gum at the same time.

The material was undoubtedly Houdini's. But what about the words? He couldn't be bothered. The text was ghostwritten. The book was intended as a slum item to be sold in theaters, a common practice of the times. At least one expert with nothing better

The master of escape has just flung off the straitjacket, which moments before bound him. The free outdoor show drew immense crowds.

Houdini attracted unprecedented crowds. Looking down during his outdoor straitjacket escape, he had this stunning view. Note that there were few women in the throng.

to do has calculated that this lobby literature brought Houdini roughly $10,000 a year.

Still, Houdini had been doing sustained writing all along—sweet notes to Bess throughout their marriage. At least daily, and sometimes two and three times day, he'd drop these billets-doux (sweet notes) declaring his love on her pillow or around the apartment for her to find. She was his sunshine, his adorable, his darling, and, curiously, he seemed always to sign them with the formal flourish of his public name: HOUDINI.

For years the handcuff king had been taking a beating from Dr. A. M. Wilson, the Kansas City editor of the leading magicians' journal, *The Sphinx*. A man of dignity and refinement, Wilson was put off by Houdini's shameless vanity and megaphone self-promotion. On the rare occasions when Houdini's name made the pages of *The Sphinx*, Wilson was careful to misspell it.

Mounting a defense, Houdini in 1906 launched a journal of his own, the ten-cent *Conjurers' Monthly Magazine*. The feud was on. He lost no time in firing off some artillery at Kansas City, pointing out with his second issue that he was already outselling *The Sphinx*.

He took aim as well at the pesky imitators who kept hanging on to his coattails. He charged that the rotten handcuff kings were a fraud upon the public and should be sent to the Bastille. Still, those who really got under Houdini's skin were the gifted ones, such as George Brindamour, a Michigan sham who billed himself as "King of all the Handcuff Artists." At times, the upstart escapist was getting better reviews than was Houdini. A fire-breathing dragon was unleashed. In snorts of flame, Brindamour was turned into Michigan pot roast.

How does a man of little formal education and hit-or-miss spelling function as a book author and editor? Houdini was smart enough to get help. He may have palmed off a ghostwriter on *The Right Way to Do Wrong,* but the magazine was another story.

It seemed to have been a family affair, with the town house on West 113th Street given as its editorial address. Everyone pitched in—even Dash in far-off London, who wrote as the official European correspondent.

The magazine shrugged off misspellings, typos, and curious grammar. While Houdini's name is not hard to find in the journal's pages, the surprise is that the self-trumpeting isn't noisier than it is.

The magazine is a great read. Houdini was a prickly editor, and its pages are bursting with life and fury and notable conjuring scholarship. To read the *Conjurers' Monthly* today, a century later, is like dining on nothing but rich desserts.

The famous Houdini–Wilson duel lasted for almost a decade. When the two mud-throwers finally met face-to-face, they burst into laughter. Embracing each other, they remained devoted friends for the rest of their lives. Houdini insisted that Wilson accept a key to his town house and regard it as his home anytime the good doctor was in New York.

Houdini had hatched a new and daring scheme that became a major plank in his legend. In preparation, he would tumble blocks of ice into his oversize bathtub and get in. He needed to practice freezing his gluteus maximus.

Then, on a bitterly cold November afternoon in 1906 in Detroit, a hole was cut in the frozen Detroit River.

Heavily manacled, hands and feet, the magician stands on the Belle Isle Bridge and peers down at the hole in the ice. He jumps. There is a splash, and he vanishes.

Two or three minutes go by. The crowd becomes nervous. Bess, unable to watch, is biting her nails back at the hotel.

Five minutes. The murmur in the crowd grows louder. No one can survive that long underwater. Houdini has drowned! The newspapermen rush off to file their stories.

A rope is thrown to the hole in the ice.

It is the splash of the rope that saves Houdini's life.

What had happened under the ice?

Escaping from the handcuffs and leg manacles was the work of moments for the handcuff king. But Houdini hadn't counted on the swift river current. It had swept him so far from the hole in the ice that he could no longer locate his exit.

Was it possible for anyone to hold his breath so long? Houdini had now been underwater for several minutes. No, quite impossible.

But he could see bubbles of air trapped between the water and the ice. With tremendous self-control, he remained calm. He floated to the ice and breathed in the trapped air.

Then, he caught sight of a splash in the water and a rope

now dangling in the current. He swam toward it. After an eight-minute ordeal, he pulled himself onto the ice, exhausted and half frozen, but very much alive.

Once again, Houdini had trumped death.

Here was the stuff of legends.

At the Temple Theater that night, and for the next two weeks, the sign went up: STANDING ROOM ONLY.

CHAPTER THIRTEEN
THE LIFE EXPECTANCY OF AN EGGSHELL

ARK TWAIN ONCE CONFESSED THAT HE COULD "remember anything, whether it had happened or not."

The hole-in-the-ice thriller you just read is one Houdini told whenever he could. I remember first reading the tale with a beating adolescent heart and a lump in my throat. I'm sure every reader made a mental note to go for those air bubbles if ever trapped under the ice.

But did it happen? Is it true?

It's true to the Houdini legend. It's as memorable a prop in the Houdini biography as the cherry tree in George Washington's. If it didn't happen, it should have.

The event unfolded exactly as Houdini said it did that November day when he leaped off the Belle Isle Bridge, except for one detail.

There was no ice floating on the river. The temperatures in Detroit around that date were well above freezing.

Houdini hocus-pocused the ice on that river. By improving on reality, he turned a routine publicity stunt into an historic three-act drama. Without the ice, the story would have had the life expectancy of a mayfly.

Houdini had the creative spark of a novelist and seemed wise to the dramatist's key question: *What if?*

What if the river had iced up?

That would have meant cutting a hole in the ice to jump through. Good theater.

What if the current had carried him away?

Splendid! The river jump would have become an underwater cliff-hanger! That was the stuff headlines were made of! And hadn't he heard as a teenager swimming in New York's East River that bubbles of air were trapped under river ice? Voilà! There was his third act.

So the curtain rose on the imperishable hole-in-the-ice legend.

Houdini was hardly a beginner in the art of mythmaking. One

of the most widely accepted conceits about the great escape artist was his fabled skill at untying ropes with his toes. Perhaps you've heard it. The cat-out-of-the-bag truth was that all he could do with his toes was get athlete's foot.

Closely guarding his secrets, Houdini set the stage for a new and jaunty legend that is alive even today. A revelation arose like a ghostly mist from Houdini's tomb in the Jewish cemetery in Queens—the shocking news that his secrets had been interred with him. Horrors! What a loss for mankind! We'd never know how he slipped out of those abrasive leg irons and handcuffs or how he walked through walls.

I believed the story myself until I came to my senses. I discovered how he walked through walls. I knew how to slip out of handcuffs; I'd done it myself. I even knew how he made the elephant disappear. And so did everyone else in the privileged world of magic, cloaked behind its barricade of secrets. The tale of Houdini's inside knowledge buried forever is divine but wonderful nonsense. "He buried no secrets," Bess Houdini declared.

Houdini understood better than anyone else that legend was good box office. As it has turned out, legend was also immortality.

Have you ever heard of such headliners as Kleppini or Cunning the Jailbreaker? They were astonishing but left no legends behind.

When asked about myths as opposed to the truth regarding the Old West, the film director John Ford said, "Shoot the legend."

Houdini was there first.

We next find Houdini sealed in a large paper bag. What was he doing there?

In every city, his cheeky challenge to escape from anything brought to the theater—"only one Test at every Performance"—put him in some wacky restraints.

In San Francisco a paper-bag manufacturer made a huge sack and defied him to escape without breaking through the paper.

Houdini was out in a flash.

In Boston, the Derby Desk Company, looking for publicity, locked the magician inside a rolltop desk. That took Houdini a little longer. In Toledo, the Marine Boiler Works riveted him inside one of its stoutest boilers. A coffin company bolted him into one of its finest wooden "overcoats."

On occasion a drunk or dippy challenger would rise from the

audience and rush to the stage with hopelessly rusted manacles that couldn't be opened with anything less than a cutting torch. One of Houdini's assistants would cheerfully escort the challenger to the wings. He would find himself thrown out of the stage door into the snow.

The most difficult escape of them all was from tarred ropes cinched around him by some high-school boys. "Hurt like hell," Houdini wrote in his diary. And he swore never to do that one again.

It is hardly a mystery why Houdini accepted these sometimes punishing challenges. He was haunted by the remark of a theater manager in St. Louis who, after business had fallen off for a week in 1908, said, "You are not worth a five-dollar bill to me." To which Houdini adds in his diary, "Is this week the first step toward oblivion?"

Great success makes great demands. Houdini discovered that he had to run as fast as he could to stay even. And audiences were as troublesome as picky eaters. They were forever demanding something new and even more dangerous.

Furthermore, imitators in ever-greater numbers were constantly nipping at his ankles. If The Great Houdini didn't accept the snorting challenges, one of the humbug Houdinis would. There was no other reason one night for the handcuff king to give the nod to a wooden box brought to the theater. Maliciously, the challengers had left it in the rain for two days. The soaked, swollen boards created one of the most difficult escapes Harry had ever endured.

These almost daily cliff-hangers, some of them quite hazardous, were a constant agony for Bess through the years. Once, lost in a crowd of ten thousand in California, Bess stood with her old friend Hattie Mooser, watching Houdini trying to escape from a straitjacket. He hung suspended by his ankles from the ninth floor of the *Oakland Tribune* building. A wind had come up, swinging Houdini about like a pendulum. "Bess took my hand and her nails dug into my palm," Mooser recalled.

Within a few years Houdini had settled into a routine of doing his upside-down straitjacket escape during the cold months and the bridge jumps in the ice-free summers.

Despite having to flit around the country and handle the demands of his stage work, he had managed to keep the *Conjurers' Monthly* publishing.

He was still a major star in Europe, with theaters continuing to clamor for him. He'd been perfecting his escape from the milk can, the lid securely bolting him underwater. He figured that would knock the lederhosen off audiences in Germany, where he was to open in September of 1908. He suspended publication of the magazine.

A new challenge was about to engage him. In Hamburg he saw his first flying machine. It was love at first sight.

He bought a Voisin biplane for five thousand dollars. Easy instructions were included. Houdini was shown how to climb into the cockpit and how to start and stop the engine. That completed his flight training. It was a world almost without experienced pilots (they numbered a couple of dozen), with schools and instructors yet to arrive on the flight scene.

On his first flight, he was barely off the ground when the bulky plane flipped over. "I smashed machine," he wrote in his diary. "Broke the propeller all to hell."

Undaunted, on a 1910 January morning in Marseille, he loaded the crated plane onto a steamship bound for Australia. He brought along a French mechanic, Antonio Brassac.

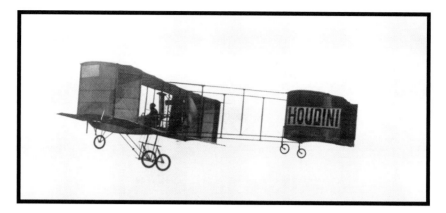

The great magician in the skies over Melbourne, making the first sustained flight in Australia, March 16, 1910.

Note that the pilot sits in front of the engine. Houdini had taught himself to fly. The Voisin had a fragile wingspan of 35 feet.

Australia had heard about the fabulous Houdini. They welcomed him with everything but a twenty-one-gun salute. After a twenty-nine day bout of seasickness, Houdini had lost weight and sprouted his first gray hairs. Bess counted only fourteen meals he'd eaten since leaving Marseille, mostly ashore at ports of call.

The Voisin was uncrated and reassembled on the outskirts of Melbourne. Another plane stood waiting for favorable weather to make the first flight into Australian skies. Built by the Wright brothers, it had been imported from America by a local mechanic named Banks. Houdini realized he was now in a race.

He was at the airfield at first light every day, remaining until showtime drew him back to the city. The winds were gusty and powerful and unrelenting. Finally, Banks's impatience moved him to action, and he roared off into the air. Almost at once a combative blast of wind caught the plane. It crashed and flopped onto its back like a dead moth. Banks walked away with a black eye. The plane was a mess.

An old hand at danger, Houdini felt cautioned, and waited. Finally, on March 16, a Friday, morning broke as if it were holding its breath. Nothing stirred but the birds. Houdini pulled his cap on backward and resolutely climbed into the cockpit. His mechanic, Brassac, spun the propeller. Behind Houdini the eight-cylinder, sixty-horsepower engine burst into a roar.

Trailing exhaust smoke like a Roman candle, the Voisin taxied down the field. At a breakneck thirty miles an hour, the wings had not fallen off, which greatly encouraged Houdini. But he was dissatisfied with the action of the elevator. He stopped to allow Brassac to make the proper adjustment to the rudder.

With his name on the tail in letters so large they could be read in faraway Singapore, Houdini released the clutch and took off again. And again. On this third poke into the Australian air, he reached an altitude of one hundred feet. The plane looked like a flying house with an outhouse tail following close behind. He was aloft among the birds for three and a half minutes.

Houdini landed on the Voisin's bicycle tires and Australia's front pages. He was famous all over again.

A day earlier, in Sydney, a twenty-year-old upstart had gotten a plane a dozen feet into the air only to tumble back to earth. He crashed into the nether world of footnotes. Unphotographed and without witnesses, the Australian's brief sojourn in the air was disqualified by the experts. The honor remained Houdini's.

The primitive airplanes of the day had the life expectancy of an eggshell. What Bess thought of Harry's waltzes with the great body snatcher can be imagined. Nevertheless, he continued his pioneering flights for a total of twenty sorties. In all photographs of Houdini in the cockpit, he's wearing a starched collar and tie. If he crashed, he may have wanted to be properly dressed for the funeral.

Soon the time came to crate up the clumsy machine and continue around the world. When he eventually reached London, his intense fever for flight had cooled down. Eventually the plane was put in storage. He never flew again.

Anyway, Houdini had a date with a sea monster.

CHAPTER FOURTEEN
UNMASKING AN ICON

IKE MIGRATING BIRDS, THE HOUDINIS FOUND themselves repeatedly crossing the Atlantic, one way or the other. While Napoleon remarked that an army travels on its stomach, the magician traveled on his back, seasick, as usual.

Fishermen working the waters off Cape Cod one September day in 1911 landed a sea monster on Long Wharf in Boston. The puzzling beast, weighing some 1,600 pounds, looked to some like a bloated octopus–tortoise mix or a grossly misshapen hard-shelled whale. The newspapers referred to the behemoth merely as a "What-is-it?"

Houdini, playing B. F. Keith's Theater in Boston, immediately saw the opportunity to cast himself in the biblical role of Jonah.

He arranged for the monster to be transported through the streets to the theater. Crowds followed to peer at this strange Great Fish. No expert stepped forward to identify the beast or to claim it for science. Marine biologists in those days were as rare as sea monsters.

The What-is-it? was surgically opened, cleaned out, and liberally painted with taxidermist's arsenic to preserve it. Metal grommets were clamped close together and laced through with a chain. That enabled the beast to be zipped up and padlocked with Houdini/Jonah inside.

Unlike the prophet, Harry was heavily burdened with handcuffs and leg irons. The theater, packed and anxious, waited.

With the creature now behind the drapes of a curtain, Houdini started to work off the manacles. But the fumes were strong and caused him to choke. He was becoming dizzy and sick. Panic gripped him. He tried to kick his way to freedom, which caused the sea beast to roll over and begin smothering him.

His assistants, sensing that something was amiss, tried to right the creature. Houdini, meanwhile, gained control of his panic. He flung off the remaining shackles and got the heck out of there.

What took Jonah three days, Houdini did in three minutes. He

The only surviving photograph of the "What-is-it?" sea monster that washed up off Cape Cod. Sewn up inside, Houdini escaped.

A rare portrait of the great mystifier. Notice his ghostly gray eyes.

was out, sweating and smiling. The audience lifted the roof. If anyone had brought a Bible for "Jonah" to autograph personally, a victorious Houdini would have been glad to oblige.

While in Boston, the proud author passed out handbills touting his inflammatory new book, his magnum opus, *The Unmasking of Robert-Houdin*. It had hardly come off the press in 1908 when magicians came after Houdini with scalping knives. The fearless author had taken the brightest icon of magic, the modernist French magician from whom Houdini had adapted his own name, and vaporized him. He revealed Jean Eugène Robert-Houdin to be a common liar, a hoaxer, a thief of others' secrets, and "an ignoramus in certain lines of conjuring."

The book is dazzling with riches, while at the same time it is petty, sanctimonious, insolent, sneering, and tormented. It is also astonishingly hypocritical.

Houdini had been collecting magicians' advertisements and other historic paper from the day he first landed in England. The book is a feast of photographs, of old engravings and playbills. The text, however, is the work of an assassin.

Houdini flew into a rage when he discovered that the autobiography of his great French idol had been ghostwritten. "Alas, my golden dreams! My investigations brought forth a mere pretender, a man who waxed great on the brainwork of others."

Furthermore, Robert-Houdin was a man of "supreme egotism." He had usurped the honor of being the father of modern magic, said Harry. That loving cup belonged to a German recluse with a knotty first name, Wiljalba Frikell. And the Frenchman's skill at sleight of hand was a joke.

But the unkindest cut of them all came when Harry cited opinions of contemporaries that the man he had idolized was a showman, indeed, but a rotten magician!

With these charges, Harry Houdini threw a boomerang that circled around and clouted him. Magicians were not amused by Harry's attempt to trash the deified Robert-Houdin. It wasn't long before they gleefully pointed out that Harry's own books, including *The Unmasking of Robert-Houdin*, were ghostwritten in whole or in part. It was true. While Harry could write a cogent sentence, he needed help with his spelling and his grammar, which was, at times, as bumpy as a country road. He hired ink-stained wretches to help out.

It must be said that Harry Houdini himself "waxed great" on

the trick inventions of others, reserving credit as often as not for himself. He adapted needle swallowing, handcuff escapes, and the sub trunk from the brainwork of earlier wonder workers.

The great French wizard was a shrinking violet compared to Harry and his steamroller of an ego, flattening everything before it. Houdini's cocky pride and unblushing airs, laid end to end, would circle the earth, with vanities left over.

Finally, back to the unkindest cut of all: the charge that Robert-Houdin was an inept magician. Guess what his contemporaries had to say about Harry Houdini once he became famous?

"Great showman. *Rotten magician.*"

Great success rattles and befuddles the conjuring community. Like a cow's tail, jealousy follows closely behind. With the publication of *The Unmasking*, Houdini's fellow wand wavers began to wave war clubs, machetes, and battle axes. "He couldn't escape from a cracker box." "Unscrupulous." "Inferior." Like righteous assassins, they gave the handcuff king the works. "That barstid Houdini!" "A bad-mannered child." Some of what they had to say was even true.

As I write this, a book has landed on my desk collecting the scorn slung at Houdini throughout the years. One illusion builder, whose wife billed herself as Minerva, the Handcuff Queen, claimed that Houdini had put acid in the water barrel she planned to escape from. A New York magic dealer recalled with a snort that Houdini, enraged to see his eight-by-ten-inch photo on display with those of other magicians, returned to replace it with a giant portrait, a dozen times larger. The vaudeville headliner was driven to outshine and diminish his competitors.

With curare-tipped arrows, the grudging critics are still on the hunt. They are hugely outnumbered by the devoted quietly going about their worship.

It is anyone's guess why Harry turned on his father figure of a mentor and teenage inspiration. And just about everyone has taken a stab at the answer.

I think this. Each field has its great icon. Einstein in science. Picasso in art. Edison in invention.

There wasn't room for two icons in magic. Robert-Houdin had to go.

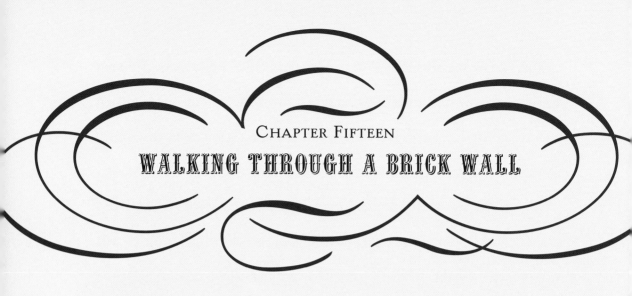

CHAPTER FIFTEEN
WALKING THROUGH A BRICK WALL

T HE SHORT ATTENTION SPAN OF AUDIENCES IS notorious. Today's sensation is tomorrow's burnt toast. Houdini couldn't ignore what he was seeing beyond the footlights. Empty seats.

The handcuff act had run out of gas. Meanwhile, cookie-cutter escape artists abounded. As Houdini expressed it, handcuff kings could be found on "the pushcarts."

He junked the manacle act, concentrating on the needle trick, the straitjacket escape, challenges from the audience, and the killer trunk trick. To be sure, there was always a plant salted in the audience, someone with leg irons or other restraints. If no one showed up to challenge Houdini, the confederate leaped to his feet.

Bess's onstage burdens had lightened. She now needed to be before the footlights only for Metamorphosis, which she could do in her sleep—and, more than once, even when she was sick.

Harry and Bess could smile now when they remembered their starving days in Chicago when a big-time booking came their way. Bess had been almost too sick to move, but when she learned how much money they were offered, she slapped some rouge on her sick-pale face. Harry flagged a cab, and the next thing feverish and aching Bess knew, she was crawling inside the dark sub trunk.

In the summer of 1912 the Houdinis were booked into New York's top-flight theater, Hammerstein's Roof Garden. Unfortunately, a sea monster hadn't washed up to accommodate Houdini. The escape artist needed an event to rouse the sophisticated New York newspapers. They had always regarded the handcuff king as something of a public nuisance. The reporters weren't impressed by real royalty, let alone a sawdust king from the dime museums.

Houdini came up with an idea that would make journalistic eyes spin. He'd weigh down a wooden packing case with hundreds of pounds of scrap iron to sink it. Then, heavily manacled, head to foot, he'd get inside with the junk. The box would be lowered into the East River.

All Houdini had to figure out was a way to get out before the confounded box drowned him.

He let the newspapers know the madness he was planning. They regarded it as an offer they couldn't refuse and sent out their scribes.

A crowd was waiting when Houdini invited the reporters to thump and examine the box and then nail the lid down over him. They were getting ready to bang away with hammers when the cops showed up.

"What do you think you're doing?"

"I'm The Great Houdini," said The Great Houdini, in all likelihood.

"I don't care if you're the Great Spirit's first cousin, you're not going to break your neck on public property."

Never at a loss, Houdini hailed a passing tugboat. The packing box, Houdini, and the scribes went aboard.

Once out in the harbor, beyond reach of the interfering locals, a heavily manacled Houdini was lifted into the box of junk. The reporters eagerly nailed him inside. Ropes were wrapped around the whole contraption, which was then dropped over the side. It sank nicely, with a rope attached like an umbilical cord.

Thirty seconds passed.

Fifty-three seconds passed.

Houdini must have figured out a way to escape, because he came bobbing up through the water. He showed the reporters a big Houdini grin. They cheered and scribbled notes for the next editions of their papers.

Fifty-three seconds? The mystery is what took Houdini so long.

Houdini was booked in Europe for the next three years. He and Bess had just arrived in Copenhagen to find a cable waiting from the United States.

Houdini had spent his entire adult life thumbing his nose at death. It would be surprising if he hadn't come to feel eternal and excused from the common destiny. He had the Grim Reaper buffaloed.

When he read the cable, he burst into tears and fainted.

His mother had died.

When he came to, he told Bess to repack. They'd catch the next ship back to the States.

He was subject to arrest. Danish law did not tolerate the

breaking of a contract. One of the show's company took the fall for Harry until the circumstances could be convincingly explained. Meanwhile, Harry and Bess had slipped onto a train to Hamburg and the docks.

Houdini was inconsolable, not for the next weeks, but for the rest of his life. Once back in New York, he lingered day after day at his mother's grave. Her face paralyzed by a stroke, she was unable to speak any last words. Houdini was haunted by what she must have struggled to say to him.

How Bess fared under his torrents of despair can only be imagined. His grief seemed touched with madness. As if Mrs. Weiss cried out to him from every room, he impulsively put the house on West 113th Street up for sale. He wrote poems by the ream to his mother. He had new stationery printed, edged in black. Ever the devoted wife, Bess comforted him as best she could without a degree in psychiatry. She must have wondered if a tormented Harry would carry on this way if she were to die.

Eventually, he was able to pull himself together—enough to function. The house, fortunately, had failed to sell, and he just as impulsively took it off the market. But his ambition had been interred with his mother.

Listlessly returning to Europe, he picked up his contracts where they had been interrupted.

He bought a secret from an English magician and distracted himself from dark thoughts by fiddling around with the idea. It evolved into a masterpiece he called Walking Through a Brick Wall.

In 1914 he introduced the feat on the stage of Hammerstein's Roof Garden, the theater where he now hung his hat when in New York. A large carpet was laid over the stage. Before the seated audience, a company of masons went to work building a solid brick-and-mortar wall. It ran ten feet long and, when finished, eight feet tall. One end faced the audience. Volunteers stood on the carpet and surrounded the wall, alert for hanky-panky.

Houdini slipped into a white smock and stood against one wall as if before a firing squad. A three-fold screen was placed around him, with another one on the other side of the wall. He raised his hands into view. Clipping his words as if he were

The *Boston Globe* published this accurate sketch of the brick wall Houdini walked through on the evening of August 1, 1914. At first, even magicians were baffled. Eventually, they figured it out.

This never-before-published photograph does *not* show Houdini dancing. Denver turned out in caps and bowler hats in 1923 to see the King of Escapes tightly buckled inside a straitjacket. He was out in a flash.

sending a telegram, he called out, "Here I am."

His hands vanished. "Now . . . I'm . . . going."

His hands reappeared on the other side of the wall. "Now I'm on the other side."

The second screen was snatched away and there, indeed, stood the Elusive American, as the newspapers had begun to call him.

Next day, the feat was on New York's lips. Wrote the theatrical paper *Billboard*, "The wonder of the age. . . . The audience sat spellbound for fully two minutes after the feat was accomplished. They were too dumbfounded to applaud."

Houdini was back in the legend business. He came to be known as the Man Who Walks Through Walls. And soon he would upstage even that nickname.

Chapter Sixteen
ONE ELEPHANT TO GO

IN EUROPE HOUDINI HAD TRAVELED WITH EVERY-thing but the kitchen sink. His needle trick packed small. His straitjacket fit inside the sub trunk with room left over for Bess's hats. Nevertheless, he dragged along trunks of manacles, historical treasures he was forever buying for his collections, and as already mentioned, a special bookcase that held a travel-ing library. He was never without something to read.

It may have been a tactical mistake in France to take advantage of a railway bargain when the Houdinis needed to pay only third-class fares if they'd be willing to travel second class.

That is the likely source of the scorn still expressed inside the world of rabbit pullers that Harry was so cheap he traveled second class. There was much in Houdini's behavior to invite a razzing, but counting pennies like a miser was not one of them.

On a return trip to New York in 1914, the seas were mercifully calm, and Houdini had his picture taken with a fellow passenger, former president Theodore Roosevelt. I would find it hard to believe the president was traveling in steerage along with Houdini.

The picture of the two famous men is a curiosity: Unseen is that they were standing with a clutch of other travelers. Never one to suffer rivals, the magician had everyone airbrushed out of the photo except the prez and himself. For a while, the picture became the centerpiece of his personal publicity.

World War I had broken out. Houdini, now forty-three years old, turned up at the army recruiting office, ready to fight the Germans.

The army chased him out of the office. He started a new career doing magic tricks for the troops. A favorite mystery was called the Miser's Dream, still widely performed today. The conjuror plucks coins out of thin air and pinches them off ears and the ends of noses.

Houdini did the trick with $5 gold pieces. Then he added a flair unprecedented in the chronicles of magic—he tossed those coins to soldiers about to embark for Europe. It has been calculated that he cheerfully pitched away more than $7,000 in gold pieces.

Houdini was merciless toward his wand-waving competitors. They kept stealing his best stuff. He hardly had time to catch his breath after walking through the wall when a fly-by-night magic outfit began selling the secret for fifty cents. Imitators were already on the loose doing his milk-can escape.

It's surprising, then, around the turn of the century, that he sought the presidency of the young Society of American Magicians. He won, and was tireless in making the sleepy organization come alive. It's still breathing robustly today, the closest we have to a trade organization.

Many years later, it was discovered that several magicians on the skids were tucked into Harry's payroll. His impulse was to be generous and paternal toward magicians who posed no threat.

Had Houdini looked into a crystal ball in good working order, he would have seen that he was about to become a movie star. But his mind was on elephants. Specifically, how to make one disappear.

It was 1918, and Houdini was booked into the enormous New York Hippodrome, a theater holding more than five thousand patrons. With the announcement that he intended to vanish a 10,000-pound Asian elephant, he filled every seat.

A fellow magician supplied him with a promising modus operandi, a secret Houdini bought on the spot.

On the evening of January 7, Houdini strode onto the stage. Wearing a black frock coat, a stiff collar, and a white cravat, he was only slightly better dressed than the elephant who came trotting out. Named Jeannie, she wore a festive baby blue ribbon around her neck and sported a timepiece on her ankle.

She gave Houdini a kiss with her trunk, waved good-bye to the audience, and marched into a wheeled box raised some two feet off the stage. At any rate, Jeannie couldn't have gone through a trap in the floor since the Hippodrome stage was built over a vast swimming pool used in water numbers.

After a few playful remarks, Houdini clapped his hands together as if to strike sparks. The doors of the cabinet were thrown open. The elephant was gone! Vanished!

Houdini again made headlines when he made an elephant disappear. If it went up his sleeve, he wasn't saying.

Even today magicians disagree on how he did it and offer conflicting methods. Mirrors? Double walls? Black art? One of the guesses is bound to be right—but which?

One thing is certain. The elephant didn't go up Houdini's sleeve.

Chapter Seventeen
THE MOVIE STAR

I T DIDN'T TAKE THE NOSE OF A BLOODHOUND TO sniff out the scent of a villain creeping up on the theater scene. Here and there a movie house was opening. People were going to the flickers.

Houdini saw earlier than most that vaudeville was on its way out and movies were on their way in. It was time for a career move. He'd become a movie star.

That he was a man of action in every sense was never in dispute. He immediately sat down with an ex-vaudevillian who'd made a couple of films and affixed his box-office name to a contract. He hammered out a deal that would be the envy of any actor today: $1,500 a week and *one half of the film's profits!*

The magician was especially committed, for the project would keep The Great Houdini alive on film for generations to come. Movies would make him immortal.

Using a film stage in Yonkers, New York, he shot a fifteen-part serial called *The Master Mystery*. It had more cliff-hangers than the New Jersey Palisades.

Houdini plays an undercover agent, Quentin Locke, who uncovers a plan by a sinister organization to steal the inventions of others. Sound familiar? And Locke—what else would Harry call himself?

At the end of the first episode, Houdini is left bound up and hanging from a couple of hooks. Locke turns into a regular Houdini and escapes. At the end of the next episode, he's cinched up in a straitjacket.

The plot gets as tangled as a fishing line. But it hardly matters, for the whole clambake is only to exploit Houdini's headline escapes. Coming next week: the packing-box-thrown-in-the-river escape.

Houdini's acting looks better than it is only because his adversary, a mechanical man, is so much stiffer. It's the first "robot" ever to appear on film. This killer bag of bolts looks as though it was made of tin cans, grocery store boxes, and library paste. Its googly eyes have the gaze of frozen Ping-Pong balls.

As an actor, Houdini was as stiff and earnest as his three-inch starched collars. Only occasionally, when he flashed a smile, did he appear relaxed. Whatever his stage charisma, it eluded the camera.

With Bess on the set, Houdini appeared to be uncomfortable in the romantic scenes. Sometimes she'd have to clear out, particularly when Harry was obliged to do a scene with the movie bad girl. The vamp's name was one of the chief glories of the film— De Luxe Dora.

The long serial played on Saturday afternoons to kids in short pants. They could hardly wait to get outside and tie one another up in ropes and play Houdini.

True to Hollywood tradition, Houdini had to sue the producer for $33,000 in profits owed him.

Harry made a two-picture deal with Paramount–Artcraft, as the studio was called in its early silent days. The Houdinis moved to sunny California. They had a reunion with the kid vaudevillian Harry had given a name to in their medicine-show days. The kid had now grown up and was the big movie star Buster Keaton.

The magician rented a bungalow in Hollywood, where he

began scribbling notes for an exposé of carnival geeks, from fire walkers to sword swallowers. It would eventually appear in 1922 under the distinguished imprint of E. P. Dutton as *Miracle Mongers and Their Methods*. Magicians still consult it.

The first feature-length film to come forth from the Hollywood sojourn was a thriller named *The Grim Game*. It featured an airborne Houdini doing some wing walking and making a leap from one plane to another. Houdini insisted on doing his own stunts since, as he put it, he was the best stunt man in the business. And that was largely true.

In *The Grim Game*, two planes came flying over the beach at Santa Monica, California, with a third, the camera plane, following and shooting from above. The two aircraft were stacked, one above the other. Then accidentally, the lower plane rose on a gust of sea wind. Its propeller ripped into the plane with Houdini on the wing. Both planes went spiraling down, leveled off, and crashed in a bean field.

The camera kept turning. The script was revised to include the heart-thumping crack-up.

Houdini walked away without a scratch. He was, in fact, miles

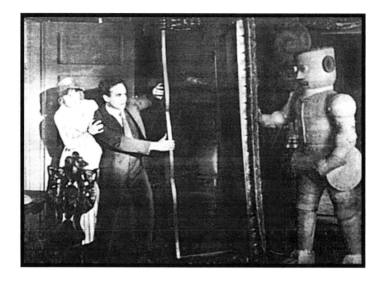

In a 1918 film called *The Master Mystery*, Houdini meets the first robot in motion picture history. If the mechanical man's movements were lifelike, it was little wonder. There was a gent inside. Some regarded the robot as a better actor than the star.

Presumably frozen for a hundred years, Houdini thaws out for his 1921 movie *The Man from Beyond*. Despite the film's abundance of escapes, audiences found the concoction beyond belief.

JESSE L. LASKY
PRESENTS
HOUDINI
IN
"THE GRIM GAME"
BY ARTHUR B. REEVE AND JOHN GRAY
DIRECTED BY IRVIN WILLAT
Morgan
A PARAMOUNT-ARTCRAFT PICTURE

For Houdini in 1919, being a movie star was the grimmest game of all. His soon-to-be-created film company would fail. In this movie, after he dropped from one Curtis Canuck to another, the two planes collided. Both crash-landed safely. Houdini walked away without a scratch—a stunt man had been doubling for him.

away. A broken wrist from an earlier scene had grounded him. A stunt double had taken the fall for him. In the retelling, Houdini airbrushed him out.

The next film, *Terror Island*, was made on Catalina Island off the southern California coast. The plots for Houdini films were now set in cement. All were the same. Houdini would be put in jeopardy and escape every several minutes. All else, including the romance, was garnish.

The movies plastered Houdini's name on gaudy billboards around the world. He saw movie publicity as a happy by-product that would otherwise have cost him huge sums for personal promotion.

But the movies were not making anyone rich. Houdini was failing to come across as a movie hero with dash and derring-do. In live performance, there was always the very real risk that he would be hurt or even killed. In the movies, the only risk was that a woman would sit in front of you wearing a large hat with peacock feathers.

And what of trick photography? Audiences were suspicious.

When Paramount–Artcraft declined to renew Houdini's contract, he started his own film company.

The first of those independent films broke the mold. *The Man from Beyond* was the first of the genre featuring creatures frozen in the past who defrost—still alive. The creature in this case was Houdini, fallen into an Arctic deep freeze one hundred years before. In the film, he thaws out to meet a young woman, a look-alike of a girlfriend he left behind a century earlier.

Houdini spent eighteen weeks shooting the movie in New York State in the Lake Placid area and at Niagara Falls—which was commandeered as a prop for a daring rough-water rescue.

Critics loved the rescue but had reservations about the rest of the goings-on. A few years later Houdini starred himself in *Haldane of the Secret Service*. This time the critics had no doubts: The picture was an absurdity. It not only lost his money, but embarrassingly, Houdini had persuaded friends to invest their own savings in his doomed production.

The movie fever that had gripped him vanished. He let theater managers know that his retirement from the stage was greatly exaggerated. He collapsed his production company and returned to vaudeville in order to recoup his losses.

His movie failures didn't go to waste. With broader fame, he was able to inflate his fees. He commanded $3,000 to $3,500 a week in 1920s money, far exceeding in a week what many men earned in a year.

For many years, Houdini had kept an eye on the flimflam artists who had largely taken over the Spiritualism movement. He had collected an enormous library on ghost hoaxers and their methods.

The time had come for action.

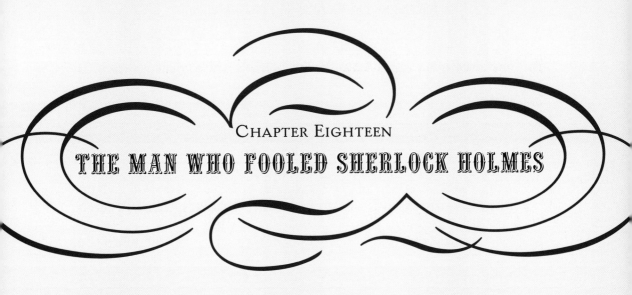

CHAPTER EIGHTEEN
THE MAN WHO FOOLED SHERLOCK HOLMES

HOUDINI RECALLED HIS MEDICINE-SHOW DAYS when, almost dead broke, he'd filled theaters by making ghosts speak from their graves. Asked questions, spirits eagerly whispered answers in Harry's ear or scribbled them out in chalk on sealed school slates. It would be too much to expect anyone to notice that the ghosts all wrote in Houdini's handwriting and made his own spelling errors.

"To me it was a lark," he later wrote.

The mystifier had used parlor tricks, but the audiences believed he was truly in touch with the dead. Houdini saw as never before that audiences collaborated in their own deception. Naive and uninformed, they embraced the supernatural as the only explanation for the strange events happening before their eyes. Short of exposing his methods, Houdini discovered that even intelligent people refused to be wised up. They insisted on the divine right to be wrong.

Houdini didn't mind fooling people but deceiving them affected his conscience. He realized the depravity of "trifling with the hallowed reverence" of those mourning the dead. At that point in his travels, as I have recounted, he quit the ghost trade.

But the spirits clung to Houdini like a bad cough.

The First World War, with its battlefield dead, re-energized Spiritualism. In what came to be called séances, grieving family and friends of the fallen would solemnly hold hands in a circle around a table. They'd sit in the dark, singing hymns and hoping to receive messages "from the other side." It was one thing to talk to ghosts—anyone could do that. It was quite another matter if the spirits answered back.

Success depended on the powers of the leader, or the séance medium. Usually a woman, the medium would go into a trace and beckon the desired spirit.

Houdini regarded séances as theater. A show. But with the

passing of his mother, he experienced the pain underlying the yearning to speak again with the beloved dead. While he had no patience with psychic hoaxers, he kept an open mind. Perhaps there was the genuine article out there in the dark.

That wild hope sustained him. If he could contact his mother, she would at last be able to speak to him as she lay dying in his absence—final words locked within by her facial paralysis. What had she tried to say? The question tortured him.

He attended séance after séance—hundreds—both in the United States and in England. He learned of a talented ghost raiser in London who was able to produce the barefooted apparition of the poet Dante. Alas, in the séance darkness, an anonymous skeptic had scattered tacks on the floor. Dante went howling and leaping unpoetically out of the room.

Houdini tracked down George Rennan, a medium in Cleveland, who coaxed ghost voices out of a megaphone for a dollar per ghost. The handcuff king had come prepared with lampblack in his coat pocket. In examining the megaphone, he managed to smudge the mouthpiece with the black powder. When the lights came up following the séance, the medium had black rings around his mouth.

Protested Rennan, "I have been a medium for forty years, and I have never been exposed."

"Well," said Houdini, "you are now."

Tracking down an honest medium in the ghost business was going to require more than a Greek holding up a lantern.

During this time Houdini struck up a warm friendship with a Spiritualist as famous as Houdini himself. The author of the Sherlock Holmes stories, Sir Arthur Conan Doyle, had seen Houdini make an astonishing escape after being shackled underwater in a glass tank. Given Sir Arthur's mind fix, one can easily imagine the sort of conversation that followed.

"My dear Houdini, I know how you made your escape."

"Do you?" replied the mystifier.

"Elementary, sir! You have the power to dematerialize yourself. It's a clear demonstration of solid through solid. You passed through the water and glass and then materialized yourself outside the tank."

Houdini managed to keep from bursting into laughter. He couldn't dematerialize a flea. Still, he knew that Sir Arthur, a committed Spiritualist, was in dead earnest.

London, 1920, when Houdini and Sir Arthur Conan Doyle, creator of Sherlock Holmes, had smiles and pleasant words for each other. Later, they would shoot verbal darts.

Houdini was not in the habit of drinking tea through his ear. He's exposing the talking teakettle used by spirit fakirs to produce wispy voices of the dead. A savvy assistant sat in a nearby room whispering into a transmitter. An induction coil concealed in the base of the kettle picked up the broadcast and directed it to a telephone receiver hidden in the spout, where it was amplified. The electronics were primitive, but they fooled the true believers.

The two celebrities maintained a correspondence, in which Houdini tried unsuccessfully to open Conan Doyle's eyes without exposing his own, closely guarded secrets. How, he wondered, could the creator of the world's most brilliant and subtle detective be so easily taken in by a magic trick? The answer seemed to lie deep, for the big man with the shaggy mustache had lost a son in the war. His Spiritualism was grief in disguise, as it so often was. He and Lady Doyle claimed to have had six conversations with their dead son.

The author's wife regarded herself as a medium. One afternoon, with the shades pulled, Houdini and the Conan Doyles sat around a séance table. In an experiment of "automatic writing," the medium held a pencil over a sheet of paper and waited for the spirit of Houdini's mother to guide it.

Before long Lady Doyle was "seized by a Spirit." Immediately the pencil came alive in her fingers. It flew over fifteen pages of spirit messages from Cecilia Weiss to her son Ehrich.

The Conan Doyles were delighted with the success of the séance. Houdini sat solemnly quiet.

He felt both disappointed and affronted. The messages were absurdly flawed. The opening image Cecilia Weiss presumably sent from the beyond was strange indeed—for the Jewish wife of a rabbi. It was the sign of the Christian cross.

Houdini had no doubt that Lady Doyle was sincere. The pencil had been guided, he thought, by her fanciful convictions and imagination. The spirit writing she took down was in perfect English. It was not a language Houdini's mother spoke. She would have addressed her son in Yiddish or German. And she would have mentioned that it was the afternoon of her birthday.

He could hardly tell Lady Doyle that the spirit writing she had produced was fifteen pages of nonsense.

With his researches now far along, Houdini kicked off his one-man crusade to expose the fakirs. He knew he was going to run into a buzz saw of believers resenting his intrusion into their occult fantasy world. He girded himself for trouble.

It was mid-nineteenth century, when ghost rappings launched the Spiritualism madness in upstate New York. Two very young farm girls in Hydesville, while lying in bed one night, decided to frighten their mother downstairs. They tied a piece of string around an apple and bounced the McIntosh along the floor. Their terrified mother below was certain that haunts were trying to communicate with her and told the neighbors. Word spread with the speed of sound.

The Fox Sisters, as they came to be known, discovered that they didn't need the apple. They could crack their big toes inside their shoes—loudly. One crack for no, three for yes. The binary language of Spiritualism was born.

People from everywhere flocked to see the uncanny Fox Sisters. The girls, ages eight and six, liked the attention as well as the money that now came falling down on them like autumn leaves. Their big toes were making them a fortune. The child Spiritualists kept their mouths shut.

But late in life they tired of the sham and came clean. The rappings, they confessed, were bunk. The only spirits the girls knew came in a bottle and smelled like whiskey. Both had taken to strong drink.

But the revelation came too late. True believers shrugged off the confessions: The Fox Sisters were drunkards, and they were lying. They were just making mischief. The believers went on unshaken and firmly believing.

Houdini's declaration of war began with a lecture exposing the methods used by the ghost wranglers. Always the showman, he staged the revelations with drama and conviction and even humor.

He'd invite several volunteers to join him on the stage. In order to duplicate the darkness of the séance, he pulled black velvet hoods over their heads. Everyone held hands and touched feet around a table. Seconds later—surprise! Tambourines shimmered and banged. Handbells rang and flew into the air.

As the spirits went about their tricks, bewildering the hooded volunteers, the audience burst into chuckles. In plain sight they had watched Houdini pulling all the psychic bunk.

They had seen how cleverly he'd secretly freed one hand to shake the tambourine. Wearing an open-toed sock, he'd withdrawn a foot from his shoe. He'd gripped the handle of the handbell with his toes and rung it like a town crier.

A favorite dodge was to tie together two school slates, face-to-face. The volunteers would ask the spirits questions only to discover the answers on the slates. Moments earlier, before the hooded volunteers but in full view of the audience, Houdini had shown how he'd switched the blank slates for prepared ones.

In due time, Houdini was offering $5,000 to any spirit medium who could pull off a psychic caper that he could not duplicate. The money went unclaimed.

He quickly learned that spirit mediums in Boston were sticking pins in wax dolls to hasten his death. "Houdini will die within a year!" crowed a medium's irate associate named Walter.

Houdini shrugged off the bloodthirsty prediction. If it should happen, he shot back, mark it up to coincidence.

The most painful casualty of Houdini's crusade was the loss of Conan Doyle's close friendship. The man behind Sherlock Holmes was immovable. He had even produced for the world to see "spirit photographs" that had come into his possession. A lucky photographer had happened upon a bearded goblin eight inches tall and four fairies aglow in the English woods and snapped their pictures. Once published, the photos were recognized as magazine illustrations trimmed out and moved into the forest by jokester girls with a camera.

Despite Houdini's revelations, he couldn't beat down the belief held by many, including Conan Doyle, that he himself possessed supernatural powers—he just refused to admit it.

A moment of tender sadness is recalled by Houdini after a conversation with the greatest French actress of the day, Sarah Bernhardt. She had lost a leg.

"Houdini, you do such marvelous things. Couldn't you—could you bring back my leg for me?"

I looked at her, startled, and failing to see any mischievous sparkle in her eyes replied:

"Good heavens, madame, certainly not . . . You know my powers are limited and you are actually asking me to do the impossible."

"Yes," she said as she leaned closer to me, "but you do the impossible."

CHAPTER NINETEEN
THE PHANTOM FOLLIES

I HAVE A HANDBILL IN RED TYPE FROM THE 1920s advertising Houdini's appearance with his spook-busting show in a strange Texas venue—the Klan Auditorium. He would be in town only one night and would answer the burning question "Can the Dead Speak to the Living?"

This booking is strange. What was the Jewish Houdini doing on the viciously anti-Semitic turf of the Ku Klux Klan? Did the klansmen in their white sheets mistake him, as others did, for an Italian? But they were equal opportunity hate mavens—they lusted for the scalps of Italian Catholics as well.

And why was Houdini, now almost fifty years old and world famous, knocking himself out doing one-night stands? (That is to say, he was playing in a different city almost every night. The time-saver of air travel didn't yet exist.) In a 1924 letter from Denison, Texas, he sends his performance dates as mail addresses to his old friends the Mooser sisters:

Denver, Oct. 21

The next night—Laramie, Wyoming.

The next night—Pocatello, Idaho.

A two-day jump to—Oakland, Calif.

The next night—Fresno, Calif. Oct. 26

When did Bess have time to get laundry done in those pre–wash-and-wear days? On a grinding lecture and show schedule like that, when does one sleep?

I can tell you from personal experience as a teenage professor of magic that you sometimes sleep sitting up or catch a few winks on the lid of a theater trunk while waiting for the curtain to rise. This is a young man's game. It is life in a cement mixer.

It wasn't that Houdini needed the money, though he emptied his pockets to buy expensive books, historic documents, Lincoln autographs, and treasures that interested him, such as Edgar Allan Poe's writing desk. His 5,000-book collection had become so large that he was obliged to put a full-time librarian in New York on his payroll.

The answer to his toil is that he was born running. He seemed incapable of restrained interest and halfway enthusiasms. He was driven to become the world's greatest magician or none at all. When human flight caught his attention, he ate and slept airplanes. He gobbled up books like a starved intellectual. Now he was consumed by his new mission—to wise up the public to the menace of occult flimflam.

So impassioned was he that a couple of years later, in 1926, he proposed a law before a committee of the House of Representatives to make illegal such fortune-telling hustles as palmistry, tea-leaf reading, phrenology, astrology, crystal gazing, and other delusional pastimes. When a congressman prodded him for his opinion on astrology, popular then as now, Houdini left no doubt. "I do not believe in astrology. They cannot tell from a chunk of mud millions of miles away what is going to happen to me."

His proposed law was rejected. He had not factored in the poet Schiller's observation, "Against stupidity the very gods themselves contend in vain."

The attacks on Houdini were now flying in from every direction. In one séance after the other, outraged spirits charged that he was a drunkard, a drug addict, and "that he kept a secret harem." Mediums began to sue for defamation and for big money. Houdini turned the suits over to his lawyer and continued his mission at full speed.

He rather liked a phenomenon who hit New York calling himself the Spaniard with X-ray Eyes. The man's sudden fame arose from his "psychic ability" to see through solids. He could, for example, read messages locked inside a silver box. With equal ease, he could look through the hinged cover of a pocket watch and see the time that had been set.

The magician in Houdini immediately saw how the Spaniard, Joaquin Argamasilla, was pulling off his swindles. He advised the young man to come clean and stop claiming psychic powers. Argamasilla refused. Houdini then exposed the imposter's sleight-of-hand trickery, and the Spaniard dematerialized. It was believed that he materialized sometime later in Madrid, his fifteen minutes of fame exhausted.

In 1924 Houdini published his adventures in the ghost trade in a substantial book called *A Magician Among the Spirits*. He made

An extremely rare and curious handbill. While on a tour shaking his fist at humbug spirits, a graying and Jewish Houdini was booked into the anti-Semitic Ku Klux Klan auditorium in Fort Worth. Didn't the rabble-rousers know? Didn't Houdini know?

Ghost for sale! This page from the 1928 Thayer Magic Manufacturing catalog in Los Angeles offers a hand that raps out yes and no messages. For a few bucks more you could buy a trumpet that speaks and taps "sitters on the heads." Big spenders could opt for an upscale version of the talking teakettle—a $75 bronze vase. Hidden inside, an early telephone system enabled an assistant in another room to simulate a spirit's voice and answer questions. Fooled the gullible.

Mina "Margery" Crandon, the prima donna of ghost raisers, slips Houdini the evil eye. Seething over the magician's exposure of her spirit flimflams, she predicted that he would be dead within a year. Came close.

Margery in action. Here, during a séance, ghost essence pours from her ear. Believers called it "ectoplasm." Skeptics called it cotton yardage.

horse meat of the whole company of séance hustlers. A compulsive clipper of newspaper items, Houdini reported such news stories as the spirit who advised wealthy clients to invest in a fly-by-night stock he was floating. And there was the young woman so befuddled by ghosts that she fell in love with one. She took her own life in order to join her beloved in the spirit world.

That same year, but too late to be included in his book, Houdini encountered his most cunning and talented spook adventurer—Margery. Blond, blue-eyed, and voluptuous as a Valkyrie on a diet, she was the superstar of mediums. She was sometimes referred to as the Witch of Beacon Hill.

The wife of a Boston doctor who was mad about Spiritualism, Mrs. Crandon—Margery—was creating great excitement with her playbill of spirit happenings. Tables routinely waltzed about in the dark, messages came through in five languages, bells jingled, and the wonderful Margery had even materialized a live spirit pigeon to flutter around the room. Her séances were truly theaters of the absurd.

Imitating established religions with their priesthoods, the Spiritualists too had their clergy. Because they supposedly had direct contacts in the Great Beyond, they were called familiars. The familiars had one thing in common: They were invisible except to the medium.

Margery's familiar was a sarcastic, foul-mouthed presence named Walter—the same Walter who had put a spell on Houdini, promising that the magician would be dead within a year.

Walter was adept at tipping over tables and throwing objects around the room. Margery was adept at ringing electric bells in locked boxes and producing fluffy "ectoplasm"—ghost essence.

This white excretion would come flowing like lava out of her mouth or ear or other body orifices. What was the stuff? It was never examined. "Don't you dare touch it!" Walter was apt to snarl. "Pinch off a bit of ectoplasm, and Margery will die!"

I have seen photographs, and as often as not the ghost essence looks like something bought on sale at a yardage store. Silk? Twisted muslin dipped in phosphorous to make it glow in the dark? When taking human form, as ectoplasm sometimes did in the shape of hands, it looked like a very bad case of running ear-wax. After Houdini's death, it was such an ectoplasmic hand that Sir Arthur Conan Doyle, in a letter to Bess, assumed had strangled

Harry as punishment for his hostility.

Houdini was drawn into the Margery sorcery when *Scientific American* magazine declared her to be genuine and Walter the real thing. Houdini rushed to Boston to have a look for himself.

A series of séances was arranged. It is astonishing that the scientists didn't think to ask their eyewitness to the Great Unknown for cosmic details. "Walter," they might have enquired, "did St. Peter greet you at the Pearly Gates? What does he look like? Did you really grow wings?"

Houdini was too savvy to buy the theatrics. He quickly realized that Walter was smoke and mirrors. Margery was confidently lowering her voice and tossing out vulgarities. Margery was Walter.

Houdini had secretly freed one of his own hands during an early séance, and guess what accidentally brushed by his finger? Margery's head. She was dropping it below the edge of the table so that "Walter" could tip the furniture over.

Later she tried to cover by explaining she had dropped a hairpin.

Again, Houdini realized, Margery had used her head when Walter tossed a megaphone across the room. It was an old trick. She had first managed to get the megaphone onto her head, like a dunce cap, and then given it a toss. The bell ringing was child's play.

Privately, Margery's husband offered Houdini $10,000 not to expose his wife's parlor tricks. He didn't know the handcuff king was not for sale at any price.

After conferring with Houdini, *Scientific American* withdrew its seal of approval on Margery.

Walter got in the last word. "Houdini, you son of a bitch, get the hell out of here and don't come back!"

In his diary, Houdini composed Margery's professional epitaph. "She was sure resourceful and unscrupulous."

But Margery was not finished. Her pack of bedazzled true believers stuck by her. She was defiant even in old age, confessing nothing, insisting that she was the real thing.

Margery's success hardened Houdini's long-held observation that otherwise intelligent people can be duped into believing anything, no matter how absurd. Ectoplasm! Talking teakettles! Tables clattering around like Spanish dancers!

Houdini's old enemy, now friend, Dr. A. M. Wilson, editor of the conjuror's magazine *The Sphinx*, wrote him in part, "Why could not the dear departed communicate direct with their relatives and friends? Why talk, or rap, or write or materialize through a medium, the majority of whom are ignorant men and woman, though shrewd and cunning . . . ?"

I don't believe Houdini would have been surprised at Margery's ascent from the ashes in today's séance parlors—television. This is where the new Spiritualism lives. Here, Margery's imitators use common magicians' tricks, one called cold reading, to fish out information from the bereaved. "I'm getting a message from the voice of a woman. I'm getting the letter J . . . Jennifer? Jane?"

"Could that be my darling aunt, Josephine?" volunteers the dupe.

"Your aunt Josephine asks you to put aside your grief. . . ."

Now that the unreluctant dead has been summoned, the medium pursues the cold reading, improvising a gossipy message—again dodging the cosmic questions.

I have just consulted a magician's supply catalogue from the heyday of Spiritualism with a thirty-page section on séance tricks for sale. You could buy floating tables, talking teakettles and trumpets, crystal balls, mind-reading scams, trick slates to receive ghost messages, luminous paint by the gallon, and complete instructions and equipment for a one-person séance. Ten dollars.

Spooks aside, Houdini was still a practicing magician. He was spending a lot of his professional life underwater in a perilous illusion of his own devising. It was called the Chinese Water Torture Cell.

With his ankles clamped in heavy wooden stocks, he'd be hauled upside down and then dropped headfirst into a tank with a heavy glass front panel. The water he displaced would cascade over the sides. In fact, the container was closely fitted to his measurements, something like a custom-made suit.

Quickly, a curtain was whipped around the torture tank. Seconds would pass. Assistants stood by with axes, to burst the tank if Houdini should run into trouble.

And then—*voilà!* Houdini's head popped through the curtains like a champagne cork. He was free!

The escape was a 1912 sensation! Houdini was to perform this marvel once or twice a day for the rest of his life. He had few imitators. The escape didn't baffle magicians; it scared them.

As a famous Broadway magician, the late Doug Henning, said publicly, "If you want to appreciate Houdini's genius, try doing his escapes."

While Houdini was forever fiddling with new ideas for escapes, he seems to have recognized that the Torture Cell was his masterpiece.

It must have surprised him that he might soon be tempting death in a most foolhardy way.

He was going to be buried alive.

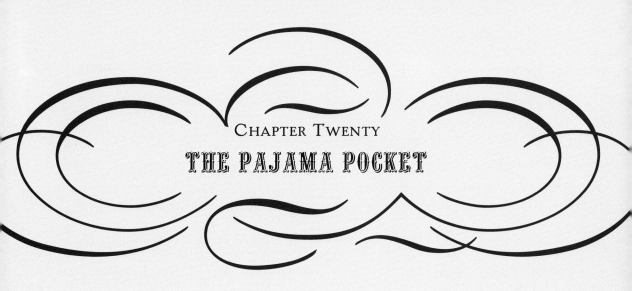

CHAPTER TWENTY

THE PAJAMA POCKET

DEATH SEEMED NEVER FAR FROM HOUDINI'S MIND. He visited cemeteries around the world the way others spend a Sunday in the park. He was drawn especially to the graves of magicians. When he found the tombstones fallen into disrepair, he often paid to have them restored. Always, he left generous bouquets of flowers.

He made solemn pacts with some fourteen people, starting with Bess, to attempt to reach one another with a secret message after each death. Bess kept her message firmly memorized and absolutely secret.

Two in the pact soon died, including a magician almost as famous in England at the time as Houdini—The Great Lafayette.

Houdini had given his friend a dog, to which Lafayette was devoted. In an Edinburgh theater fire, the illusionist had dashed backstage to rescue the dog and perished.

Despite Houdini's furious denunciations of occult charades, his eagerness to believe persisted. There might be something genuine lurking beneath all the humbug, if, like cobwebs, the tricksters could be swept aside.

At Lafayette's grave, Houdini was startled when a flower vase fell over—not once, but twice. "Laf?" Was that his old friend trying to reach out to him?

Bess advised him not to get carried away. She thought she may have brushed by the vase with her long skirt.

Returning to New York from a lecture tour, Houdini began to prepare for a lifelong dream—a full evening production. A two-and-a-half hour wonder show.

In the midst of these preparations, like a sleeping volcano that could be expected to awaken regularly, Houdini erupted one May night in 1926. He had learned that a scam artist was moving in on his territory.

Claiming to be an Egyptian dervish with occult powers, Rahman

Bey was going to out-Houdini Houdini. Inside a coffin, he would put himself in a trance while buried under shovelfuls of dirt—and survive in a state of suspended animation.

Houdini had tried out a buried-alive stunt in Los Angeles some fifteen years before, and sworn off. He had come close to panic as the earth kept caving in on him while he attempted to make his escape from a coffin buried six feet under.

But he couldn't allow this fakir to upstage him. Houdini would go Rahman Bey one better—and survive the burial without calling upon the fanciful powers of the ancients. And he'd do the whole thing underwater to make it largely visible and scam proof.

In due time, he was laid inside a galvanized iron coffin, soldered watertight by tinsmiths. Afloat in the swimming pool of New York's Hotel Shelton, the iron casket was submerged by volunteers standing on the top.

Houdini had a telephone and an alarm bell at hand in case the telephone failed. How long could he keep breathing the miserly air supply surrounding him? Everyone on the outside waited for the alarm bell to sound off. Doctors had estimated that only enough oxygen was available to last three or four minutes before Houdini would black out.

Ninety minutes later, Houdini calmly telephoned to be brought to the surface. In his upstart demonstration, Rahman Bey had yelled for help in fifty-odd minutes. How had Houdini almost doubled his time?

No Egyptian trance. No supernatural powers. "By natural means," Houdini declared firmly.

He had prepared by practicing slow, shallow breathing to conserve oxygen. And the doctors, he had found, were wrong: There was a good deal of air in a coffin. Whether there was additional magician's trickery involved, the handcuff king wasn't saying.

Houdini let nothing with publicity value go to waste. He had colorful lithographs printed that shouted EGYPTIAN FAKIRS OUT-DONE! The art showed Houdini inside a coffin leaning against a pyramid, about to be buried alive. As a dress rehearsal for his own death, it didn't come close.

It was 1926, and what Bess thought of starting another tour now that she had reached the age of fifty, she left no clue. Houdini bought her a beautiful dress for her birthday. She was still jumping in and out of the Metamorphosis sub trunk as she had done when she was eighteen. She still kept their books and paid the bills. And by remote control while on the road, she still managed the huge home on West 113th Street.

In the fall the Houdinis took their new show on the road. It featured needle swallowing, escape from the Chinese Torture Cell, and a demonstration of séance tricks that the famous Margery had used to hoodwink the suckers.

The tour started badly. In Providence, Rhode Island, Bess was felled by a bad case of ptomaine poisoning. Harry worked the show around her absence and then rushed back to the hotel. He had hired a nurse but stayed up with the wretched Bess half the night. Without any sleep, he caught an early train to New York to meet with his attorney. Lawsuits from prickly mediums now brought claims of more than a million dollars.

Houdini moved the complicated show to Albany, where, as soon as she was able to travel, Bess followed with the nurse.

With the press of obligations, Houdini had gone thirty-six hours without sleep.

During the first Albany performance, the exhausted magician

slipped his feet through the mahogany stocks in preparation for his second-act closer. As he was being hauled into the air by block and tackle to be lowered into the Torture Cell, he let out a cry of pain.

With the audience watching, he was lowered. He had twice broken a wrist when he was making movies and now had an idea what had happened. He hobbled toward the footlights and asked if there was a doctor present.

There was, and he determined that Houdini had broken a bone in his ankle and needed to go to the hospital for X-rays.

But Houdini refused to stop the show. The doctor improvised a splint and left the stage.

Houdini scrapped the Torture Cell and closed the act with the needle trick, standing on one foot. He was able to rest during intermission, but when the curtain rose on the third act, he was back on his feet.

Only after finishing the show did he go to the hospital, where the bone was set and his ankle put in a cast. He was advised to take an enforced rest for a few weeks, but this was show business and he had to move on. And anyway, he never coddled himself. He was invincible, wasn't he? Had he shut down filming when he broke his wrist bones? In this escape business of his, he was accustomed to bruises, torn muscles, cuts, and assorted aches and pains.

Pushing on proved to be a death sentence.

It's doubtful that Walter, Margery's wispy familiar, crossed his mind even as the pain kept Harry from sleeping. "Houdini will be dead within a year," the snarling spirit had predicted.

The year had passed, but not by much. Was there a margin of error in this ghostly clairvoyance?

The show moved on to Schenectady and then to Montreal, Quebec, where it opened for a week's run at the Princess Theater on Monday, October 17, 1926.

Houdini had agreed to give a lecture at prestigious McGill University on the subject of occult superstition and fraud. He knocked the college kids dead. What pleasure he felt at his achievement—this drop-out grammar-school kid now addressing a university audience—is not hard to imagine.

Sitting with two friends, one an amateur boxer, a student artist had been drawing a sketch of Houdini as he spoke. After the lecture, the student brought the drawing to the lectern. Houdini was pleased and invited him and his friends to visit him backstage after the evening performance.

The three young men turned up early the next afternoon. Lying on his dressing-room couch to rest his ankle, Houdini was going through his pile of mail. His duties as the national president of the Society of American Magicians were conducted by letter. In addition, great stacks of mail came in daily from, among others, ghost groupies who cussed him out.

In his lecture at the university, Houdini had claimed that as a result of regular exercise and a life without drink or tobacco, he had retained his physical youth and was able to absorb a hard blow to his body with complete ease.

The student boxer stepped forward, asking, "Is it true? Can you take a punch to the body?"

Houdini was only half paying attention as he separated personal mail from the usual time wasters. "Sure," he muttered.

The kid asked about testing him now and Houdini, distracted, seemed to give an absentminded nod. The boxer then hauled off and let the escape king have it—a blow to the abdomen.

Not just one. Four rapid fists before Houdini was able to stop him.

Plunged headfirst into the Chinese Water Torture illusion, Houdini discovered a way to escape. But it was as dangerous as it was ingenious and not many contemporary magicians have chosen to duplicate this showstopper.

The episode passed. The boys left and Houdini continued with his mail. His abdomen felt merely bruised. The pain would go away.

It didn't. Still, he got through the evening performance and the Saturday matinee. But the pains were growing more severe, and he was breaking out into cold sweats.

The show company had a train to catch. Houdini was to open in Detroit Sunday evening. He was so ill on the train that Bess had a wire sent for a physician to meet the train.

Houdini's temperature on arrival was 102 degrees. The doctor said he had appendicitis and wanted to take him to the hospital. The escape king scoffed. He was Houdini! Bess fell into tears.

The theater was sold out. He was now so weak that he had to be helped into his tuxedo. If all those people had come to see Houdini, Houdini would appear! His temperature was 104.

Once the spotlight hit him, he seemed restored. He ripped off his shirtsleeves, as he always did, to prove he was hiding nothing up his arms. Then he plucked silver dollars out of thin air. Alarm clocks vanished and appeared across the stage, ringing from the ends of ribbons. The magician, "suave and smiling," tried to produce yards of colored silks from a fishbowl but found himself to be too weak to lift them. An assistant stepped in.

With his broken ankle, the Chinese Water Torture trick was cut. Resting during intermissions, Houdini was able to summon reserve strength, and he finished the show.

He refused to go to the hospital for surgery, as the doctor was now insisting. Bess, still not well herself, was becoming hysterical. At the hotel, he phoned New York to talk to his brother Dash and to his own physician there, who conferred with the hotel doctor. Houdini, the invincible, rejected their joint advice. He'd escape from this medical crisis as he had from everything else. Dash caught the next train to Detroit.

But on the verge of collapse, his resistance gave way. He was rushed to Grace Hospital, where his ruptured appendix was removed. But Houdini had waited too long. Gangrene of the appendix had developed. Peritonitis was furiously advanced. Antibiotics hadn't yet been invented. Houdini wasn't going to live.

Today, some doctors scoff at the notion that blows to the midsection could reach the well-protected appendix. They believe it had burst without any outside help.

Houdini's impending death was front-page news, and the hospital issued bulletins on his condition twice a day. Then came Halloween. October 31, 1926.

Night had not yet fallen, with its ghosts and goblins. In his hospital room, Houdini motioned his brother a little closer and closed his eyes. "I'm tired of fighting, Dash."

Ill herself, Bess had taken the room next to his. She now returned to his side. Houdini's eyes cracked open again. He took a last look at his wife of more than thirty years of sawdust and limelight. He took a last breath.

Houdini was dead.

As a final memento, Dash removed the pocket of his brother's pajamas.

When Ehrich Weiss departed, he was accompanied by his closest companion and his greatest illusion, The Great Houdini.

Chapter Twenty-One
POSTMORTEM

THE HOUDINI STORY BY NO MEANS ENDS WITH HIS entombment beside his parents in the Machpelah Cemetery in Queens. You'll recall that he had left a secret word or code with Bess. If she should receive a spirit message from him, it would repeat the secret.

Bess let stand a $10,000 reward to any medium who could make a genuine contact and reveal the secret message. The occult folks made so many greedy blind stabs that after two years and attending many dead-end séances, Bess canceled the offer.

She sold the house on West 113th Street, with its many rooms of their youth, and eventually moved to California in 1935. There, as a young teenage conjuror, I came to know her and to visit her rustic home in Laurel Canyon. To one side of the wide veranda, in a stainless-steel rectangle surrounded by gravel, an eternal flame flickered. I had never seen one before and recall staring at it with a feeling of awe and privilege.

Formally, we called her Madame Houdini; informally, Bess. She became a sort of den mother to us young enthusiasts. She gave me a couple of pictures of the great magician, being published here for the first time.

During her last years, she turned her business affairs over to a benign, savvy, and distinguished-looking former crystal gazer with a waxed mustache, a trimmed beard, and a dashing walking stick. Dr. Edward Saint, a name and an academic degree he bestowed upon himself, devoted his energies to preventing Houdini from becoming one of the forgotten Olympians. The handcuff king became one of the rare showmen with a publicity man promoting him years after going "on tour—forever," as Bess chose to regard Harry's death.

It was Ed Saint who arranged a special séance on the roof of the Knickerbocker Hotel in Hollywood on the tenth anniversary of Harry's death. Bess Houdini gathered with some two hundred distinguished magicians and guests on a chilly Halloween night with a hope of receiving a sign from the famous ghost muckraker. A radio hookup would broadcast the séance around the world.

Her platinum hair almost incandescent in the moody night air, tiny Bess sat enthroned in a great carved chair. Her eyes were heavy and funereal with mascara. Before her, as the focus of attention, were gathered curious props to tempt the ghost of the great Harry.

A pair of locked handcuffs, of course. If Houdini's spirit could pop them open, it would be proof. Surely that would be a convincer that the dead do return, and throw cynics into confusion.

As backup, a school slate had been added, upon which he might scratch out a message. Perhaps he'd rather announce his presence by firing the pistol loaded with blanks. A handbell to ring? Above all, the great mystifier would be obliged to utter the secret code words known only to Bess. A silver séance trumpet, shaped like a megaphone, had been thoughtfully provided to amplify Houdini's ghostly voice.

At the stroke of eight thirty, the séance got under way with a scratchy phonograph playing the opening music from the magician's stage performances.

"Houdini, are you here?" intoned Ed Saint, who was running the show. With his bald head glistening and his immaculately trimmed beard now fluttering with intensity, he summoned and begged and invoked.

"Manifest yourself, Harry. Give us a sign. Shoot the gun. Unlock the handcuffs!"

A tense Bess waited. The world waited. One could hear faint traffic sounds from Hollywood Boulevard below.

"Manifest yourself! Write on the slate." Dr. Saint cajoled and entreated. Finally, with high emotion, he began to beg. "Do something, Harry. Please! Make yourself known to us!"

But not a sign from Harry. Not a snap of the handcuffs or a jingle of the bell.

Years later, Bess would recall Ed Saint's noble efforts. "He invoked and he invoked—good lord, how that man invoked!"

Harry was a no-show.

The eternal light that Bess had kept burning for the past ten years was aglow in its shrine installed on the table. Now Bess rose to say, "Houdini hasn't appeared. I am convinced that the dead cannot return. It is over, finished."

She reverently turned the switch and the eternal light went dark. The séance was over. "My last hope is gone," she said. "The spirits do not exist."

Of course—but wait!

At almost the same moment, the skies rumbled and a cloudburst struck, as if Harry had thrown a thunderbolt from the heavens.

Bess was soon to hear from an English woman who wrote regarding Harry, "I'm sorry he couldn't go to you, but he was having tea with me at the time."

Bess had grown weary of the fantasy world of spirit mediums. Before she died of a heart attack in 1943, on a train crossing the California desert at Needles (how curious!), she issued a statement. She swore that she would absolutely *not*, positively *not*, make any attempt herself to return from the dead. Ghosts didn't walk or talk. It was all hogwash.

She unburdened herself of the secret words Houdini had given her. They were "Rosabell," a song title from their youth, and "believe" spelled out in magician's code. She had no further use for them.

On Halloween night, 1936, on the rooftop of Hollywood's Knickerbocker Hotel, Bess Houdini makes her final attempt to raise the ghostly spirit of the great magician. A megaphone was provided for Harry to speak through, while a bell stood waiting should he prefer to ring. The neatly bearded gent standing to Bess's left is her manager, Ed Saint. "He invoked and he invoked—good lord, how that man invoked!" Alas, Houdini didn't oblige. As the séance broke up in disappointment, a cloudburst struck as if he had thrown a thunderbolt from the heavens.

Master of the ghostly revels during the final Houdini séance, Dr. Edward Saint was neither a doctor nor a saint. His name was Charles David Meyers. He had been a Midwest "Sees-All—Knows-All—Tells-All" crystal gazer before going legit and taking over as conservator of the Houdini legacy. Without his efforts, much of the escape artist's playbills, clippings, and photographs would have been lost. I met him several times and was properly impressed. He was devoted to Bess. They may have married; no one knows for sure.

I think the Houdinis would be amazed to discover that they are not buried together. It's impossible to imagine that he, so wedded to Bess, would have allowed himself to be separated in death.

Houdini had defied religious convention when he cleared the way for a graven image to be installed at his gravesite in Queens's Machpelah Jewish cemetery—a bust of himself. Aware that only those of his own faith could be laid to rest beside him, wouldn't he have managed an exception to the rules—again? He was, after all, *Houdini!* The most luminous star in Queens, alive or dead. A catch for Machpelah.

A contrary fate appeared in the person of Bess's sister, Marie. The two sisters were traveling together on a last train ride across the California desert. Bess was on oxygen. Marie claimed that Bess had reembraced her original religion an hour or so before she died. On that assumption, Bess was given a Catholic burial in New England. The devoted lovers of almost half a century were drawn apart for separate and lonely eternities.

After so many years of retirement from the public scene, Houdini should be yesterday's newspapers. Far from it. Many kids today may not recall the governor of their states, but the name Houdini rings a loud séance bell. He was the man who could escape from everything but the common cold.

While a few contemporary magicians scoff at Houdini's abilities as a magician, all concede that he had genius as a showman. When the escapist dangled upside down in a straitjacket from the top of an office building, a stampede to the box office followed. That was showmanship.

There is hardly a major river in the United States or Western Europe that Houdini, heavily manacled, never jumped into. Showmanship. And on stage he had the commanding confidence of a field marshal. Among his powers was the ability to take an obscure trifle such as the Indian Needle trick and turn it into a masterpiece. Audiences adored him.

But was he a rotten magician, as some within the fraternity still insist? Compared with whom?

Today's kings of cards leave Harry in the dust. Breathtaking new sleights and flourishes have come into being since his day. Seventeen-year-old kids, still wet behind their theatrical ears, could fool the socks off him as well as his great contemporaries, Howard Thurston and Harry Blackstone.

Bad? Harry?

Bold and daring, he didn't become a icon by fumbling his tricks. How difficult was it to vanish an elephant or walk through a wall? Not very—take my word for it. Bad magicians, no matter how skilled, are tedious and boring. It's an absurd rap to lay on Houdini.

Naturally, Houdini has not escaped the sharp eye of psychiatry. His passion for escaping from straitjackets, milk cans, and sea monsters suggests the birth drama revisited. Those wishing to pursue these interpretations will find Dr. Bernard Meyer's book in the following bibliography both well written and a page turner.

The mother lode of Houdini's life story was published in 1928 in the biography I've referred to in chapter two, written by Harold Kellock with the collaboration of Bess Houdini. As she most certainly read the manuscript, why did she allow some of the legendary but fanciful stories of Harry's early years to go through to the printer? Picking up needles with his eyelids, for example.

I think she had embraced Houdini's mythmaking. She had heard his tales so often she may have come to believe them. And who can resist a good story?

Collecting Houdiniana is a recent phenomenon. I can remember a Saturday afternoon in the 1930s at Thayer's Magic Studio, where every week the Los Angeles conjurors gathered to talk secrets. Bess had grown tired of lugging around so much tonnage of Harry's notebooks, pictures, and old correspondence. She allowed Thayer to sell off Houdini letters at fifty cents each. I don't remember a rush for them. In fact, I don't remember anyone buying anything. Today, a Houdini letter is valued at $1,000 to $3,000, depending on what he had to say.

A magician and friend, Tom Conley, recalls as a boy being left to amuse himself at the magic studio's trash pile. While his father joined his colleagues, Tom pulled an autographed picture of the escape king out of the junk heap, now published here. He also fished out Houdini's stage diagram for one of his watery escapes, specifying that the water be heated to a comfortable ninety degrees.

No one valued the relics. Trash. But that was then.

As a biographer, I found Houdini to be both a pleasure and a trial. To enter the world of the handcuff king was to find yourself in a house of mirrors. Conflicting information, rubber facts, and howling nonsense are reflected everywhere you look. When was he *really* born? Don't ask him. In *The Right Way to Do Wrong* he states that he was born in 1873. He wasn't. His birth certificate says 1874. He seemed unable to resist tampering with his great invention—Houdini.

Why he altered the very day and month of his birth is a different conundrum. Here, he has confounded his biographers. One writer put forward the notion that Harry, not knowing the day and month of his birth, charmingly plucked one out of thin air.

The obvious struck some few, including me. In calculating Ehrich's birth date from the ancient Jewish calendar to the modern one, Rabbi Weiss or another hand blundered. Such errors were not uncommon.

And Houdini's scrappy ego! He plastered his name on everything from huge billboards to a tiny self-portrait engraved inside Bess's wedding band. Not even his pajamas, as we have seen, were safe from his restless pride.

Still, without that hurricane of an ego, Houdini would have joined other great magicians as they ambled into obscurity. Ever hear of Herrmann the Great? Keller? Thurston? Once headliners each one, now footnotes.

Houdini has arisen from his grave like a mist of ectoplasm to

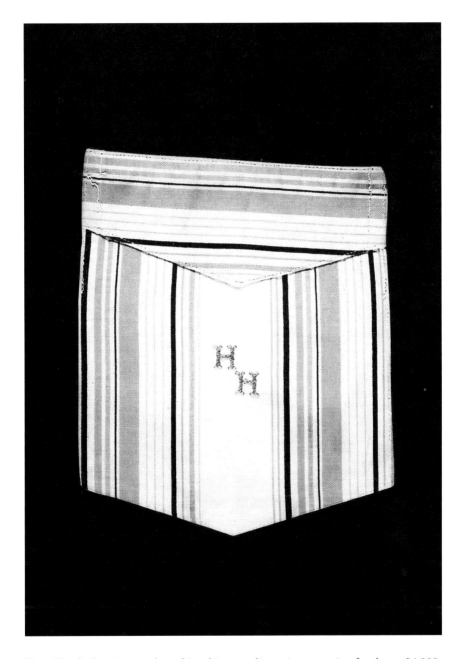

Even Houdini's pajama pocket achieved immortality, going at auction for almost $4,000.

become one of the immortals. His sidewalk star blazes up from the Hollywood Walk of Fame. More astonishing than his famous trunk trick, he pulled off a metamorphosis from a dime-museum trickster to the greatest magician in history.

Not bad for a kid who used to roll up his cuffs and say, "There ain't nothing up my sleeves."

DIGGING AROUND IN HOUDINI'S PAST

I HAD ACCESS TO A GREAT DEAL OF HOUDINI MATERIAL published privately within the magic fraternity. Supplementing that were several books published through the decades for the general public. Here is a selection of major texts that I have drawn upon from both worlds.

Brandon, Ruth. *The Life and Many Deaths of Harry Houdini.* New York. Random House, 1993. A detailed and intimate portrait of the escape king's life, with an emphasis on the Jewish factors that figure importantly in his rise from poverty to stardom.

Christopher, Milbourne. *Houdini: The Untold Story.* New York: Thomas Y. Crowell, 1969. A highly readable biography written by a skilled magician.

————. *The Illustrated History of Magic.* New York: Thomas Y. Crowell, 1973. Riches for the magic buff, with a generous chapter on the escape artist. Choice.

Culliton, Patrick. *Houdini Unlocked.* Los Angeles: Kieran Press, 1997. A valuable two-volume treasury of original Houdiniana texts, snapshots, and photographs of all the principle players in the magician's life. Published in a limited edition for Houdini cultists. I was constantly turning these pages to double-check details.

Gibson, Walter B. *The Original Houdini Scrapbook.* New York: Sterling Publishing, 1977. As the title promises, a random collection of old advertisements, letters and pictures.

———. *Houdini's Escapes and Magic.* New York: Blue Ribbon Books, 1930. I exposed none of Houdini's secrets in this biography. Magicians resent exposures merely to satisfying passing curiosity. How then does one learn the how-it's-dones to become a magician? By troubling to seek out books such as this, for the serious inquirer.

Gresham, William Lindsay. *Houdini: The Man Who Walked Through Walls.* New York: Henry Holt, 1959. A swift and bemused telling by a novelist of the Houdini story, and the first to reveal the handcuff king's Budapest birthplace. High marks.

Henning, Doug. *Houdini: His Legend and His Magic.* New York: Warner Books, 1977. A deft handling of the Houdini story, largely written by Charles Reynolds. An oversize paperback, it stands out for its charm and style and wonderful visuals, some in color.

Houdini, Harry, editor. *[The] Conjurers' Monthly Magazine.* New York: The Conjurers' Monthly Magazine Publishing Corp., 1906–1908.

Houdini, Harry. *A Magician Among the Spirits.* New York: Harper & Brothers, 1924. Interesting.

———. *Miracle Mongers and Their Methods.* New York: E. P. Dutton and Co., 1920.

———. *The Right Way to Do Wrong.* Boston: Self-published, 1906. Ghostwritten.

———. *The Unmasking of Robert-Houdin.* New York: Publishers Printing Co., 1908.

Kellock, Harold. *Houdini: His Life-Story*. New York: Harcourt, Brace and Company, 1928. The book that launched a thousand magicians. A romantic mixture of fact and legend.

Meyer, Bernard C., M.D. *Houdini: A Mind in Chains. A Psychoanalytic Portrait*. New York: E. P. Dutton and Co., 1976.

Rauscher, William. *The Houdini Code Mystery*. Pasadena, Calif.: Mike Caveney's Magic Words, 2000. A highly specialized book that, among other matters, gathers together many of the insults thrown at Houdini.

Silverman, Kenneth. *Houdini!!! The Career of Ehrich Weiss*. New York: HarperCollins, 1996. A Pulitzer Prize-winning historian renders a scholarly and fully detailed biography of the Self-Liberator.

Steinmeyer, Jim. *Hiding the Elephant*. New York: Carroll & Graf, 2003. An inventor of stage illusions surveys all of the great ones and explains the clever methods that enable them to baffle the public. This is the book to go to for secrets. Written from profound knowledge and with a novelist's touch.

Weltman, Manny. *Houdini: Escape Into Legend, The Early Years: 1862–1900*. Van Nuys, Calif.: Finders/Seekers Enterprises, 1993. The late Mr. Weltman spent a lifetime searching out Houdiniana. A gem.

Auction catalog, Swann Galleries. Magic, sale 1911. New York. October 30, 2001.

Two contemporary magazines for insiders, with their long memories, were invaluable. They are:

Magic, The Magazine for Magicians, 6225 Harrison Drive, Las Vegas, NV 89120

Genii, The Conjurors' Magazine, 4200 Wisconsin Ave NW, Washington, DC, 20016

With gratitude and delight, the author wishes to thank many friends and a stranger or two for permission to reproduce photographs and images from their Houdini collections in this book.

Michael Claxton Collection, p. 136 (bottom); Tom Conley Collection, pp. 89 (top), 125; Patrick Culliton Collection, pp. 5, 21, 26, 63 (both photos), 72 (top), 89 (bottom), 136 (top), 148 (top), 157 (both), 169 (top), 194; *Genii, The Conjurors' Magazine* Collection, pp. 43; Library of Congress, pp. 9 (right), 14 (both), 23, 36 (both), 42 (both), 53, 72 (bottom), 78 (bottom), 98 (top), 105, 142, 148 (bottom), 149, 169 (bottom); Magic Collectors' Association, p. 104; Steve Mooser Collection, pp. 30, 118 (both), 168 (top); Norm Nielsen Collection, jacket front (also p. 185), jacket back (also p. i); Swann Auction Galleries, p. 201.

In addition, photos on pp. 9 (left), 78 (top), 98 (bottom), 124, 168 (bottom), and 195 were supplied from the author's collection.

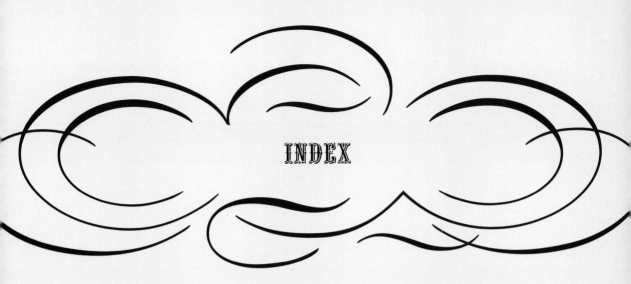

INDEX

THE RESTLESS GHOST

But wait. There's more.

Houdini's ghost is too restless to stay out of the headlines. The ink was still drying on this biography when the great magician reached up from his tomb and grabbed the public spotlight again—not once, but twice. A neat trick!

Houdini's grandnephew, George Hardeen, announced that he would have the theater star's body exhumed to determine if his famous relative had been poisoned.

The notion that spiritualists of Houdini's day made a hobby of threatening the life of the escape artist and ghost exposer has been knocking round the magic world for decades. The trouble is, no one can figure out how poison was able to burst Houdini's appendix and end his life. It's nonsense, of course.

But since believers will forever want to fetch shovels and start digging, I will save them the bother. It would have been out of character for Houdini to have passed up the opportunity for a last great escape. They may discover that the magician's coffin lies empty.

Enter William Kalush, an impassioned New York magic enthusiast. He phoned me one day and asked to see unique research material in my hands. He explained that he was preparing a Houdini biography launching the notion that Houdini was an American spy during World War I.

I told him I hadn't discovered any evidence of cloak-and-dagger in my archives. To prove it, I took down from my office wall a framed Houdini letter, typical of my holdings. Dated May 30, 1923, from Sioux City, Iowa, it began:

"Dear Hat and Folks,

"We are not coming to Frisco. Am playing Middle West as far [as] St. Louis, Mo. Must return near N.Y. for business reasons—"

At this point, Kalush interrupted to say, "Aha! That could have been spy business."

I realized at once that I was talking to a true believer. His book was rushed into print a few months after *Escape!* and the spy angle made a big splash.

Could the cloak-and-dagger conjecture be true?

No. Houdini never in his life made an important decision without conferring with his wife, Bess, and his brother Hardeen. If Hardeen knew about this secret life, as Kalush claims, so did Bess. Magicians' wives know how to keep secrets.

Why does this matter?

After Harry Houdini's death Bess had a close relationship with Ed Saint, who made it his life's work to promote the Houdini legend. Bess would have been certain to feed him the old spy story. And Saint, the world's greatest megaphone, would have shouted the news to the world. No doubt. Positively. Absolutely!

Spy? Poison? These headline grabbers would be passing bunkum were they not in the tradition that has grown up of ever-new Houdini myths and fantasies being launched as fact.

What next, Harry?

—Sid Fleischman
January, 2008

The teenaged author with Bess Houdini, in San Diego
for Magicians' Day at the World's Fair, 1936

ABOUT SID FLEISCHMAN

The cheapest crystal ball could have predicted that Sid Fleischman, the Newbery Award–winning author of *The Whipping Boy*, would someday write a biography of the hero of his youth—the immortal magician Harry Houdini.

As a teenage prestidigitator, Fleischman came to know the widowed Bess Houdini, who had retired to Southern California. In his autobiography, *The Abracadabra Kid: A Writer's Life*, he describes her as "a kind of den mother to us young West Coast magicians." She gave him photographs that now appear in these pages.

Among Sid Fleischman's celebrated comic novels, published in nineteen countries, are *The Giant Rat of Sumatra*, *Bandit's Moon*, *Disappearing Act*, *Bo & Mzzz Mad*, and *The 13th Floor: A Ghost Story*. The father of three children (one of whom is Newbery Medalist Paul Fleischman), he lives in Santa Monica, California. You can visit him online at www.sidfleischman.com.

READ ON FOR AN EXCERPT FROM SID FLEISCHMAN'S NEW BIOGRAPHY:

THE TROUBLE BEGINS AT 8

A LIFE OF MARK TWAIN IN THE WILD, WILD WEST

CHAPTER ONE
THE MAN WHO MADE FROGS FAMOUS

Mark Twain was born fully grown, with a cheap cigar clamped between his teeth.

The event took place, as far as is known, in a San Francisco hotel room sometime in the fall of 1865. The only person attending was a young newspaperman and frontier jester named Samuel Langhorne Clemens.

Who?

A person of little consequence. He was a former tramp printer, Mississippi riverboat pilot, and ink-stained scribbler who'd made a small noise in the brand-new Nevada Territory.

Sam, or even Sammy, as boyhood friends and relatives sometimes called him, sat in the light from the hotel window scratching out a comic story about a jumping frog contest. He'd discovered the bleached ribs of the story not far off, in the California Gold Rush foothills. He now set the tale in his native folk language. He gave the story fresh and whimsical orchestration. He made it art.

He rummaged around among several pen names with which he'd amused himself in the past. Newspaper humorists, such as his friends Petroleum V. Nashby and Dan De Quille, commonly hid in the shade of absurd false fronts. Should he be Josh again? Thomas J. Snodgrass? Mark Twain? How about W. Epaminondas Blab?

Mark Twain. It recalled a shouted refrain from his riverboat days, signifying a safe water depth of two fathoms, or twelve feet. He'd given the pen name a trial run on a political scribble or two, but the name had only enhanced his obscurity. He had let it molder and die.

Still, he would feel cozy under the skin of a character from his beloved Mississippi River. Maybe he'd blow on its ashes and resurrect the pseudonym. With earnest decision, a possible snort, and a flourish of his pen, he signed the piece, "By Mark Twain."

Nothing traveled fast in those days except the common cold. But once the celebrated frog of Calaveras County reached the East

Coast and was reprinted by newspapers large and small, the nation had seizures of giggles and guffaws. The merriment spread with the swiftness of a gale-force wind. The story crossed the Atlantic Ocean, and before long the English and later the French "most killed themselves laughing" as Twain reported, falling back on his Missouri drawl.

Today, we are still smiling out loud at how Smiley lost the frog-jumping contest to a stranger with a secret cache of buckshot.

Mark Twain had made the overstuffed amphibian famous. At first, the creature had grabbed the spotlight exclusively for himself. The author reacted with a bilious grunt of jealousy toward his creation. Complained Twain, "It was only the frog that was celebrated. It wasn't I."

But soon Mark Twain caught up, sprinting past the croaker to become the most famous American alive. And the funniest.

Each chomping simultaneously on the same cigar, Sam Clemens and Mark Twain conspired to write what many regard as America's greatest novels, *Adventures of Huckleberry Finn* and its companion *The Adventures of Tom Sawyer*. And that's not to mention the knockabout pages of *Life on the Mississippi* or the fanciful *The Prince and the*

Pauper, a novel about two look-alikes who exchange places, with results you can imagine. An unending carnival of movies, plays, and Broadway musicals have been spun off from Mark Twain's rowdy comedies and satires.

From under the author's full mustache, hanging like a rusted scimitar over his sharp quips, came an evergreen stream of wit. His sayings remain as perky today as when Twain first minted them. "Man is the only animal who blushes, or needs to," said he. "Cauliflower is nothing but cabbage with a college education." "Everybody complains about the weather, but nobody does anything about it."

Not bad for a barefoot boy with a prairie fire of curly red hair who was born in Florida, a Missouri village so small that Sam remembered it as "almost invisible." Halley's comet was streaking across the sky like a chalk mark the day he was born. Seventy-five years later, it came blazing back, as if by personal invitation—the day the celebrated author snubbed out his cigar and moved in with the immortals.